JUNG

A BEGINNER'S GUIDE

RUTH BERRY

Hodder & Stoughton

A MEMBER OF THE HODDER HEADLINE GROUP

Orders: please contact Bookpoint Ltd, 130 Milton Park, Abingdon, Oxon OX14 4SB.
Telephone: +44 (0)1235 827720. Fax: +44 (0)1235 400454. Lines are open 09.00–18.00,
Monday to Saturday, with a 24-hour message answering service. Details about our titles and
how to order are available at www.madaboutbooks.com

British Library Cataloguing in Publication Data: a catalogue record for this title is available from
the British Library.

ISBN 0 340 78055 X

First published 2000
Impression number   10 9
Year   2005

Artist Richard Chapman
Typeset by Transet Limited, Coventry, England.
Printed in Great Britain for Hodder & Stoughton Educational, a division of Hodder Headline,
338 Euston Road, London NW1 3BH, by Cox & Wyman Ltd, Reading, Berkshire.

Hodder Headline's policy is to use papers that are natural, renewable and recyclable products
and made from wood grown in sustainable forests. The logging and manufacturing processes
are expected to conform to the environmental regulations of the country of origin.

CONTENTS

Contents

Who was Jung?

Carl Jung was a Swiss **psychologist and psychiatrist**. He lived from 1875–1961 and he is famous because he founded a new system of psychology that he called 'analytical psychology'. Jung has gradually acquired a huge following and many therapists today are trained in the Jungian method. Much of what we know about Jung's life and work can be found in his autobiography, *Memories, Dreams Reflections*. Quotes from Jung in this, book have been taken from a translation of this title (see Further Reading), unless otherwise stated.

WHY IS JUNG'S WORK SO IMPORTANT?

A great many people have heard of Jung and many books have been written about him and his work. He was a prolific writer himself – his work stretches to over twenty volumes. Some of the ideas and terms that he coined have found their way into everyday use today, for example the words 'archetype' and 'introvert'. Jung was a great scholar, and his interests were wide-ranging, covering such areas as astrology, alchemy, archaeology and world religions. His thinking and work were based not only upon these interests, but also on his own practical experience working with people who came to see him professionally.

The system of psychology that Jung developed was very much a spiritual psychology, setting it apart from the mainstream, which tended to be rigidly **mechanistic** in outlook. Jung had a lifelong fascination with the spiritual and the **numinous**, saying that the latter was the most important aspect of his work. His interests were deliberately wide-ranging, covering many spiritual traditions, because he was trying to search for

> **KEYWORDS**
>
> **Psychologist:** scientist who studies the mind and behaviour.
>
> **Psychiatrist:** someone who studies and treats mental and nervous disorders.
>
> **Mechanistic:** view that sees a person as a machine whose behaviour is determined by physical or chemical causes.
>
> **Numinous:** awe-inspiring; indicating the presence of the divine.

truths that were common to all mankind. He believed a person's spiritual life to be of paramount importance in the healing process. A person's individual life story was the thing that mattered – Jung was interested in listening carefully to what a person had to say about this. He regarded clinical diagnoses as being useful only to the doctor,

KEYWORDS

Unconscious: parts of the mind and personality of which a person is unaware.

Psyche: the mind, soul or spirit.

for the purpose of giving him a 'certain orientation'. He did not regard them as being helpful to the patient.

Jung was born towards the end of the nineteenth century, at a time when great changes were beginning to take place in society, particularly in the field of science. Charles Darwin's (1809–1882) theory of evolution had challenged religious thinking, causing people to question the truth of what was written in the Bible. Sigmund Freud (1856–1939) was expanding people's awareness of the importance of the **unconscious** in human psychology. Even the structure of society was changing, as people began to live in smaller groups. People were searching for new truths and becoming more interested in self-knowledge.

Throughout his work, Jung stressed the importance of the unconscious. He tended to use the word **psyche**, which covered both the conscious and unconscious processes. 'Mind' on the other hand was often used to imply concern only with conscious processes. Jung insisted that the psyche is no less real than the physical world. He pointed out that everything that we are aware of is perceived and interpreted by the brain, so that we can never actually know for certain the truth about the outside world.

WHAT IS ANALYTICAL PSYCHOLOGY?

Analytical psychology is a whole system of psychology that Jung gradually developed throughout his life. His ideas came from various sources:

* from nearly sixty years, experience as a practising psychologist,

studying the experiences of his patients;

* through painstaking study of his own inner world, dreams, visions and symbols;

* by reading widely and also travelling, in order to explore the **myths** and religious beliefs of many cultures.

Jung became interested in the idea that certain common themes ran through the myths and culture of all people. This led to his idea of the **collective unconscious**, one of the central themes in Jungian teaching.

Analytical psychology has several main aspects:

* a method of therapy, aimed not only at treating mental and nervous disorders, but also at helping ordinary people to become more balanced and self-aware;

* an attempt to provide a map of the human psyche in order to understand more fully how it works;

* an exploration of the deeper aspects of human psychology through the study of religious beliefs, dreams, myths, symbols and the **paranormal**.

KEYWORDS

Myths: traditional stories that try to explain natural, social or religious ideas.

Collective unconscious: the deepest layer of the unconscious, which extends beyond the individual psyche.

Paranormal: things that cannot be explained by normal, objective methods.

Psychoanalysis: a system of psychology and method of treating mental disorders, originally developed by Freud.

Jung coined the phrase 'analytical psychology' around 1913 in order to describe his work and to distinguish it from the system of **psychoanalysis**, originally developed by Sigmund Freud.

Since Jung's death in 1961 his analysis of the human psyche has been widely recognized as an important framework for studying psychological problems. However, by his own admission, his ideas are not always easy to follow. He remarked that he could not claim to have reached any definite theory and that his work consisted of a series of different approaches.

Despite this difficulty, Jung encouraged people to experience things for themselves and where possible develop their own insights. Towards the end of his life he finally agreed to make an attempt to put some of his main ideas together in a way that was more understandable by ordinary people. The result was a book called *Man and his Symbols*, and this is a good starting point for studying Jung's ideas. The book emphasizes Jung's lifelong conviction that the inner world of the human psyche is of paramount importance and needs to be studied seriously.

JUNG'S FAMILY BACKGROUND

Jung was born in 1875 in Kesswil, Switzerland. When he was six months old his family moved to Laufen, near the Falls of the Rhine. Then they moved to Klein-Hüningen, which was at that time a village near Basel. Jung had many relations in the Church – in fact eight of his uncles were pastors. His father was a pastor in the Swiss Reformed Church, whose teachings were strongly influenced by the sixteenth-century Reformation teachings of leaders such as Calvin and Luther. The Reformed Church taught people to believe in the literal truth of the Bible, or else risk damnation. Jung's father had strong scholarly interests in classical and Oriental studies, but he accepted the teachings of his Church without question. Jung said later in life that in childhood he associated the word 'father' with reliability, but also with weakness.

Jung's mother was also rooted in the faith of the Reformed Church. However, her beliefs were more complex because her own family firmly believed in contact with the spirit world. Old pagan beliefs still held strong in the minds of people in rural Switzerland. Jung saw his mother as a dynamic and powerful person, but also as unpredictable and mysterious. His parents' marriage was not an easy one, probably because their characters and beliefs were so very different. His mother was earthy, extravert and chatty, whereas his father was scholarly and introvert. When Jung was three, his mother was hospitalized for several months with a nervous illness. When he was nine, his sister Gertrude was born, but she played little part in his childhood. Young Carl was a solitary child and liked to play alone.

The different influences from his parents probably played a part in creating a dualism that Jung recognized in himself later in life. He felt that his personality was divided into two characters which he called 'Number 1' and 'Number 2'.

* Number 1 was concerned with the external everyday world. This side of Jung was ambitious and **analytical**, looking at the world from a scientific point of view.

* Number 2 was secretive and mysterious and tended to look at things in an **intuitive** way.

A BRIEF OUTLINE OF JUNG'S CAREER

School

Jung attended a country school where he was intellectually well ahead of his classmates. He welcomed the company of other children, but close friendships were not easy for him because he was so used to playing alone. From the age of 11 he attended a school in Basel, but he was never happy there. The other boys thought him peculiar and tended to make fun of him. Not only that, he found the lessons boring and felt that they were a waste of time.

> **KEYWORDS**
>
> Analytical: studying things by breaking them down into their separate elements.
>
> Intuitive: knowing things without having to reason them out.

University

Family poverty meant that Jung could not expect to study at a more distant university, so he was admitted to Basel in 1895 after leaving school. He had wanted to study archaeology, but it was not taught at Basel, and so he chose medicine instead. This was in the family already, his paternal grandfather having been Professor of Surgery at the university until 1864. After taking his degree in medicine in 1900, he almost decided to specialize in surgery, but he had developed a strong interest in psychiatry and eventually decided to move in this direction.

First appointments

Jung became an assistant at the Burghölzli mental hospital in 1900, and in 1905 he was appointed Lecturer in Psychiatry at Zürich University. He was especially interested in the disorder then called dementia praecox but later referred to as schizophrenia. Jung left the hospital in 1909 so that he could work with private patients. He also wanted to concentrate on his research into the psychological aspects of behaviour and the inner world of the unconscious.

Recognition of his importance

In 1907 Jung met Sigmund Freud and for a number of years there was a close friendship between them. Jung became the first president of Freud's International Psychoanalytic Society and was the editor of its journal, which was the first of its kind. Eventually Jung's independent way of thinking led to a rift with Freud. He continued to develop his own school of psychology and he was eventually made president of the International General Medical Society for Psychotherapy in 1933. In 1936 when Harvard University marked its tercentenary by awarding honorary degrees to the most eminent living scientists, Jung was one of the people chosen. His reputation had grown and he had become a leader of international research work in psychology, partly because he eagerly exchanged ideas with others. Even in old age he was known as a great conversationalist who retained a wide range of information about different topics. His charismatic personality meant that he attracted a huge following.

JUNG'S PRIVATE LIFE

Jung was tall and well built, and many people found him physically attractive, especially women. He met his wife, Emma Rauschenbach, when he was just 21 and she was 16. The first time they met she was standing at the top of a staircase, and Jung had an immediate premonition that she was to be his wife. They were indeed married seven years later, in 1903, and their first child Agathe was born in 1904. Over the next ten years they had four more children – three more girls and a boy. At first they lived in rooms at the Burghölzli hospital, but in 1909 they were able to move into a newly built house on the lakeside at Kusnacht near Zürich. Jung had known from very early childhood that he wanted to live near a lake. Luckily for him, Emma was the daughter of a wealthy businessman, and this left Jung free to pursue his own interests a lot of the time.

Emma Jung worked as an analyst in the therapy practice, taking on her own patients. She also gave lectures at the Jungian institute in Zürich. She was especially interested in Arthurian legends, and made a special study of the legend of the Holy Grail. Antonia Wolff also worked alongside Jung and became his mistress from about 1911 onwards. The relationship became a complex triangular one that must have been very difficult for both the women. Jung himself fatly announced that a man needed two women – one to organize the domestic affairs and one to be stimulating to the intellect! In fact he was an incurable womanizer and had many other affairs in addition to his relationship with Antonia.

Jung outlived both his beloved women and missed them in his last years. He carved memorial stones for each of them, with Chinese inscriptions. Emma's reads 'she was the foundation of my house', and Antonia's 'she was the fragrance of the house'. He did not write a great deal about people who were close to him, probably in order to protect them.

Jung travelled extensively, visiting places as far apart as North Africa, New Mexico, Kenya, Uganda, and India. He lectured in both Britain and America. People usually described Jung as being friendly and interested, but he had odd moods when he would become preoccupied, even rude. At these times he would withdraw from society and he built himself a special retreat at Bollingen for this purpose. When the mood took him, he was totally driven by the need to indulge in creative activity or study. This meant that he sometimes hurt people or made enemies because he appeared distant.

Jung died in 1961 after a brief illness. His death was appropriately followed by a violent storm, during which lightning struck his favourite poplar tree by the lake.

✳ ✳ ✳ ✳ SUMMARY ✳ ✳ ✳ ✳

● Jung is famous because he founded a new system of psychology that he called analytical psychology.

● He regarded the spiritual and the numinous to be the most important aspects of his work and maintained that the psyche was as real as the external world.

● Jung coined the phrase 'analytical psychology' around 1913 in order to describe his work and to distinguish it from the system of psychoanalysis, developed by Freud.

● Jung saw himself as having two personalities, one analytical and the other intuitive.

● He gradually acquired a huge following and became famous all over the world, but many of his ideas were regarded with suspicion by more orthodox scientists.

● He was a charismatic man, but at times he could be moody and difficult to live with.

Jung's Early Life

2

BOYHOOD

Because Jung played alone a great deal when he was a child, he became introspective and developed a rich and imaginative inner world. His later work as an analyst and a great thinker had its roots here. Young Carl spent a lot of time pondering over philosophical and religious questions, many of which were very sophisticated for his age. His playmates were fun to be with, but he felt that they alienated him from his true self – he was only able to be truly himself when he played alone. Later in life he remarked that he felt he needed people both more and less than others did. He found people fascinating, but he also needed a lot of personal space.

In his autobiographical book, *Memories, Dreams, Reflections*, written towards the end of his life, Jung recalls various important incidents from his childhood. Some of these were to have profound effects and haunt him all his life as detailed below.

The stone

When he was aged between seven and nine, Jung often played near a wall made of large blocks of stone. He had a fascination for starting little fires in hollows in this wall. He felt that the fires were in some way sacred, and had to be kept fed so that they would burn forever. In front of the wall was a slope with a stone in it that jutted out so that you could sit on it. Jung would play a game where he would alternate between being himself sitting on the stone, and being the stone which was being sat upon. After a while he would become uncertain of reality and would stand up wondering 'who was what now'. This confusion was exciting and interesting, and was always accompanied by 'a feeling of curious and fascinating darkness'. This was one of his first experiences of the numinous, which was to become of paramount importance to him in later years. The stone, in fact, was to become the foundation of his analytical psychology.

The secret manikin

When he was about ten, Jung carved a 5 cm manikin from the end of a ruler. The manikin wore a frock coat, top hat and shiny black boots. Jung sawed him off and made him a home in a wooden pencil case, complete with a little bed for him to lie on. He added a smooth black stone from the Rhine River, which he painted to divide it into upper and lower halves. The manikin and his sacred stone were secret and Jung hid them on a beam in the attic where he was forbidden to play because the floorboards were unsafe.

Whenever he was upset or there was an undercurrent of trouble between his parents, Jung would sneak up to look at the manikin. Each time he visited, he added a tiny scroll, written upon in a secret language and bearing an important message. The secret manikin gave him a sense of power and security that was so important that he considered them to be the 'essential factor' of his boyhood. He knew that they represented an enormously important secret and this was his first real attempt to give shape to it.

Jung saw his whole life as an unfolding of 'the self-realization of the unconscious'. He felt that what is referred to as a person's 'personal myth' could express that person's inner world more precisely than science ever could. The manikin in the attic was somehow symbolic of his own inner world as a child – it was a part of his own evolving personal myth. Although in old age Jung's recollections of the external world had faded, his encounters with the 'other reality' were as vivid as ever. These were what really mattered to him and he seems to have been aware of this fact from an early age.

Jung's earliest recollected dream

When he was three or four, Jung dreamed that he was in a meadow, where he came upon a dark, stone-lined hole with steps leading down underground. He went down and there, in an underground chamber, was a wonderful golden throne. Seated upon this throne was a huge thing made of flesh, 4.5–5.5 m high and about half a metre thick. On top it had a rounded head, with a single eye gazing upwards. He was paralysed with terror and as he stood transfixed he heard his mother's voice telling him 'that is the man-eater'.

It was only years later that he realized that the thing was a phallus. The dream was oddly un-childlike and sophisticated – where had the anatomically correct phallus, sitting like some subterranean god come from? It was not until he was about fifty that he connected it with a book he read about the motif of cannibalism underlying the symbolism of the Mass. He was puzzled as to how a child could have had knowledge of things that were to fill his later years with 'stormiest passion'. Jung maintained that his intellectual life had its unconscious beginnings when he had that dream.

Jung's first experience of a neurosis

Jung describes having an early personal insight into the process of forming a neurosis. When he was 12 years old he was pushed over by another boy and banged his head. After that he began to have fainting fits whenever school or work were mentioned. He was kept off school for six months and enjoyed rambling around alone, living with nature and communing with his own inner world. All the while his pleasure was somewhat spoilt by a vague sense of guilt. Eventually, he overheard his father talking to a friend and telling him how worried he was about his son's future. Jung rushed off and immediately began to study his Latin books, struggling every few minutes to overcome giddy spells. Within a few weeks he was back at school and had the uncomfortable realization that he had engineered the whole thing himself. From then on he worked hard. As he walked to school one day he suddenly felt as if he had emerged from a dense cloud. He thought to himself 'now I am *myself*.

EDUCATION

Jung was nevertheless bored by school, feeling that it took up too much of his valuable time. Many subjects he found too easy and did very well in them. However, he objected strongly to algebra and found maths as a whole to be 'sheer terror and torture'.

Maths was sheer terror and torture.

Divinity he found 'unspeakably dull', despite his interest in religious questions. He had an 'utter incapacity' for drawing, and gymnastics was ruined for him by physical timidity and the fact that he resented people telling him how to move. Meanwhile, as he was growing up he had an enduring sense of inferiority, feeling himself to be somehow contemptible.

Between the ages of 16–19 this lengthy sense of depression slowly lifted, but he was still rather unpopular with his schoolmates. He was still struggling with his feeling of an inner split in his personality, which seemed to force him to try and live in two very different worlds at once. Partly because of this, he felt unable to decide what to study at university. He was fascinated by natural science – zoology, palaeontology, and geology. On the other hand, he felt equally drawn to comparative religion and prehistoric archaeology. Eventually he won a scholarship to study medicine at Basel University.

Being at university made Jung feel alive, and he found plenty of friends. He read books on philosophy as well as medicine, and was especially interested in the works of Kant, Neitzsche and Swedenborg. He joined the university debating society where they discussed the human soul and other interesting religious questions.

Jung felt a great wave of excitement when he first came upon a book about psychiatry, *Lehrbuch der Psychiatie*, by Richard von Krafft-Ebing. Krafft-Ebing spoke of the **subjective** nature of psychiatry, describing how the

KEYWORD

Subjective: to do with, or coming from, the self.

psychiatrist studied his patient with the whole of his own personality. Jung realized with a flash of illumination that here at last was a way in which he could integrate the two currents of his internal world. This was where science and the spiritual met.

JUNG'S INTEREST IN SPIRITUALISM

While he was at university, Jung found a small book on spiritualism and realized that the phenomena described in it were related to stories that were familiar from his childhood in the country. Such things as predictive dreams, clocks that stopped at the moment of death, ghosts and table turning fascinated him. His friends on the other hand reacted either with total disbelief, defensiveness, or even dread.

One year, when he was home for the summer holidays, an incident occurred that affected Jung profoundly. The family heard a loud crack in the dining room. Rushing through they found that their circular walnut dining table had split right across, not along a joint, but clean through the solid wood. A few weeks later another deafening cracking sound was traced to a bread knife, which lay inside the sideboard shattered into several pieces along the blade. The knife had been used at teatime and then put away as normal.

Jung and his mother both felt that there must be some underlying reason for these two strange incidents. A few weeks later he was asked to attend a seance and he decided to go along. He went on to attend regular seances on Saturday evenings. The medium, who was a young cousin of Jung's, took on the personality of a woman called Ivenes. Through Ivenes she relived past-life experiences and dramatic love affairs. Eventually Jung lost interest when he discovered that the girl had invented some of the evidence in order to impress him. But he felt that the whole experience had been important because it had further aroused his interest in the human psyche.

SCIENTIFIC THINKING AT THE TURN OF THE CENTURY

In the 1890s, when Jung was a student, psychiatry was in its infancy. People tended to see it as being related to psychical research and spiritualist ideas. These were very much in vogue at the time and the Society for Psychical Research had been founded in 1882 in Cambridge, England. At the same time, new scientific understanding of the unconscious was beginning to emerge, pioneered by Sigmund Freud. The accepted way of thinking in science was based on **positivism**, which limits knowledge to things that are directly observable. This approach goes hand-in-hand with the mechanistic view.

KEYWORDS

Positivism: a way of thinking that limits knowledge to that which is directly observable.

Philosophy: a system of learning that investigates the underlying nature and truth of knowledge and existence.

Psychotic: suffering from severe mental disorder.

The idea behind postivism is straightforward – simply describe the facts of what can be experienced and observed. Anything else is not considered to be science. Positivists also try to make general scientific laws about the ways in which phenomena are related. This approach began in the natural sciences and spread into **philosophy**. Most psychologists took a positivist stance, but meanwhile psychiatry was also developing, as people became interested in mental illnesses. It was hard to explain these illnesses by means of conventional medicine and mechanistic thinking.

BURGHÖLZLI

In 1900, Jung was appointed as an assistant at Burghölzli, a psychiatric clinic at the University of Zürich, run by Eugen Bleuler. The patients at Burghölzi were mainly **psychotic**. Jung worked here for nine years, studying the group of illnesses then known as dementia praecox, now called schizophrenia. The mechanistic outlook said that such illnesses were caused by neurological damage or organic disease. However, Freud's new ideas about the unconscious were beginning to take effect, suggesting that this might not necessarily be the case. Jung was especially interested in experimental psychology and did extensive work using word tests, whereby the doctor gave the patient a word and the patient responded with whatever came first into his or her head. If a noticeable delay occurred, then unconscious emotions were probably at work. Jung carefully noted reaction times and responses and found that he could identify **complexes** of related responses.

Jung also worked with a galvanometer, an electrical instrument that measures the electrical conductivity of the skin. This varies according to how damp the skin is – when a person is stressed it tends to be damper. The galvanometer was used as a sort of lie detector, and Jung

KEYWORD

Complexes: a related group of emotionally charged unconscious ideas.

actually managed to use this method to incriminate a nurse who had been stealing money. He later abandoned the idea of using a galvanometer because he realized that the stress level was more related to a person's *feelings* of guilt than to *actual* guilt.

In 1905, Jung was appointed as a senior doctor and lecturer in the medical faculty at the university. He gradually began to move away from experimental psychology, feeling that doctors were too keen on describing symptoms, making a diagnosis and compiling statistics – all manifestations of the mechanistic view. Jung wanted to find out what was actually going on in the minds of the mentally ill – he was not interested in labelling people.

Jung was interested in the **psychogenic** causes of mental illness. For him each patient has a story that needs to be told and this is where therapy begins. A person's symptoms will often make perfect sense in the light of their individual story. The problem is always the whole person, never the symptom alone. Jung began to explore the unconscious minds of his patients, using word association, dream analysis, or simply by endlessly and patiently talking. This is where his friendship with Freud became very important.

KEYWORDS

Psychogenic: disorders that originate with mental conditions – physical symptoms may follow.

Repressed: experiences that have been actively pushed out of the conscious mind into the unconscious.

Neurosis: minor nervous or mental disorder.

JUNG AND FREUD

In 1906, Jung sent an account of some of his findings to Freud, whose work on the unconscious interested him and seemed to confirm some of his own findings. Freud's psychoanalytic therapy was aimed at treating mental and nervous disorders. It worked with theories about the unconscious and the ways in which it interacts with the conscious mind. The therapy was based partly on a free association process very similar to Jung's work with word association. The patient was helped by this method to recall **repressed** experiences and so begin to sort out any underlying **neurosis**. Freud also worked a great deal with dreams and this aspect of his work also interested Jung.

Freud extended psychoanalysis to include a system of developmental psychology in which he described certain biologically determined phases that everyone is supposed to go through during childhood. People could get stuck at any stage and this caused problems later on in life, which would often emerge in the form of neuroses. People tended to get stuck as a result of conflicts that arose between basic biological urges and the norms for correct behaviour imposed by society. For a long time Freud insisted that these basic urges were fundamentally sexual in nature. He used the term 'libido' to describe the sexual drive that gave rise to the urges.

Freud and Jung got on especially well at first, and a kind of father–son relationship developed between them, Freud being nearly 20 years older than Jung. Freud wanted Jung to be his successor, and in 1910 he appointed him as the president of his newly formed International Psychoanalytic Society in Vienna. However, problems soon began to arise in their relationship. Freud had found out that Jung had been having an illicit affair with one of his patients and he confronted Jung disapprovingly. Jung retaliated by being hostile towards Freud, who claimed that Jung taunted him by talking incessantly about some mummified peat bog men that were being dug up in north Germany. Jung connected these with other mummified remains that had been found in cellars in Bremen, where they were staying at the time. Freud became upset and eventually fainted. Later on he explained that this was because he had felt that Jung had a death wish against him. He had hinted at this notion previously, when he had tried to analyse a dream of Jung's involving skeletons in a cellar (you can read more about this dream in Chapter 5).

Jung gradually began to formulate new theories of his own. He said that he had had reservations from the beginning about his relationship with Freud, feeling that Freud tended to put him on a pedestal. His own feelings were very intense too – he said that it was almost as if he had a teenage crush on Freud. Freud had also recognized that this intensity of feeling might end up in some sort of 'teenage rebellion'.

In 1912, Jung lectured at Fordham University in New York. Outwardly he was still struggling to be supportive towards Freud, but in fact he ended up criticizing the basic theories of psychoanalysis, saying that:

* the 'libido' should not be regarded as merely sexual, but more as a universal life force. Later he abandoned this term altogether and tended to refer to 'psychic energy';

* pleasure could come from all sorts of non-sexual sources, not merely from sexual sources, as Freud had tended to insist';

❋ adult neuroses were caused by current problems that resurrected old conflicts. These were not necessarily infantile conflicts, nor were they always sexual.

Not long after this attack, Freud and Jung met up again at a conference in Munich in 1912. Freud talked to Jung at length and felt that he had won him back into the fold. Freud then proceeded to faint again at lunch, and Jung had to carry him through into another room. Clearly Freud was deeply upset about the whole affair. The next year Jung lectured in London and talked once again about wanting to move psychoanalysis away from its narrow emphasis on sex. He coined the phrase 'analytical psychology' at this time to describe the new ideas that he was evolving and to distinguish them from psychoanalysis.

Letters between Freud and Jung became increasingly bitter and Jung accused Freud of behaving like a controlling father, intolerant towards new ideas. Sadly, in 1913, their friendship ceased altogether and before long Jung resigned his presidency of the International Psychoanalytical Society. Although the relationship between Jung and Freud did eventually end, there is no doubt that Freud was very important in helping Jung towards formulating his theories.

❋ ❋ ❋ ❋ *SUMMARY* ❋ ❋ ❋ ❋ ❋

● Jung was a solitary child and in his imaginative games he began to grapple with some of the ideas that were to fascinate him all his life.

● School largely bored him and it was not until he discovered psychiatry that he began to find his true path in life.

● He had a lifelong interest in the paranormal, which was to have profound influences upon his work.

● His work at Burghölzli brought him into contact with psychotic patients and inspired his interest in the ways in which the human personality develops.

● Freud was a very important figure in the development of Jung's ideas.

Jung's Inner World

3

JUNG'S MID-LIFE CRISIS

After the breakdown of the relationship between Freud and Jung, Jung went into a lengthy depression that nowadays would probably be called a mid-life crisis. He was 39, many of his former friends turned their backs on him and he gave up his university post. He felt a great sense of disorientation, as if he were suspended in mid-air and could not find his true path in life. His reaction was to turn away from the world for a while and withdraw into his own inner world. Dreams and fantasies became increasingly interesting to him, not only his own, but those of his patients as well. He could not understand why other doctors were so obsessed with making firm diagnoses and did not seem interested in what their patients actually had to *say*.

THE IMPORTANCE OF MYTHOLOGY

Jung had developed an interest in mythology over many years. During his time working at Burghölzli he began to realize that many myth-like themes emerged in the dreams and fantasies of the insane. Current thinking in psychiatry said that people carried daily 'residues' – images from day-to-day experiences that are consciously forgotten but are stored away in the unconscious. Jung began to wonder whether it was possible that people also carried 'archaic residues', by which he meant little snippets of inherited impressions and imagery, stored in myth-like forms. From this he began to develop his theories about the collective unconscious and archetypes.

Jung found references in mythology to heroes who went off on a 'Nekyia', or 'night-sea journey'. This was a very dangerous form of quest where the hero was likely to be swallowed up by enormous sea monsters or by an all-devouring female. For Jung this female figure seemed to represent the mother to whom we are all attached in our childhood and from whom we must eventually separate our own psyche. Sometimes the hero has to be swallowed up by a monster in order to find rebirth.

This mythical idea corresponded very closely to what was going on in Jung's own inner crisis. He seemed to live under a constant inner pressure, at times so strong that he thought he must have some serious psychic disturbance.

> **KEYWORD**
>
> Mythopoeic: to do with the making of myths.

But he also realized that the dreams and visions that were flooding through his troubled psyche were somehow connected to the ideas expressed in myths. They were the substance of what he called the **mythopoeic** imagination, which we tend to overlook in our rational age.

Such imaginative ideas are everywhere, but, as Jung had already discovered, they tend to be found mainly at the unconscious level and are often treated with dread and suspicion when they emerge into consciousness. Many people are often scared of what goes on in their own unconscious and see any investigation as being dangerous – they are afraid that they might lose control. Indeed, Jung knew all too well from his clinical work how dangerous the unconscious could be, and at times he feared that he might become psychotic like his patients. He realized that it was essential to retain a normal life within the real world in order to counterbalance his excursions into the inner world. His family and his work acted as anchors, reminding him that he was a real person and preventing him from becoming totally ungrounded. Jung was determined that he would somehow remain in control, and began to study his own crisis almost as if he were both patient and doctor at the same time. He felt lost, without a frame of reference, and so he began to look around for ways to chart his journey.

CREATIVE PLAY

Jung tried going over all the details of his childhood in order to try and find a cause for his disturbances. He did this twice over, but it seemed to get him nowhere. In the end he decided that he must be less analytical and try to submit to the impulses of his own unconscious. This had interesting results. The first thing that came into his head seemed to be a memory of a passionate interest he had had when he was about ten years old. He had endlessly used building blocks to construct little houses, castles and villages. As the memory welled up he felt very emotional and excited, so he decided to re-enact the childish phase by actually indulging in similar games. At first he felt self-conscious, but he soon found that it was a good way of really getting back in touch with the true essence of himself at that age.

Jung collected suitable stones and began to build. He made cottages, a castle, a village and a church, but he hesitated to add an actual altar within the church. Then one day, walking by the lake, he found a perfect little red stone pyramid, about 4 cm high. He was delighted, realizing that this must be the altar for his church. As he put it in position he was reminded of the phallus dream he had had when he was very little – the strange god seated upon his underground throne. He felt immensely satisfied by this.

Jung would play every afternoon until his patients arrived.

Every afternoon Jung would play until his patients arrived, and then again in the evening. For the rest of his life he used such creative play as an invaluable therapeutic tool. Whenever he came up against a mental block he would paint, or work with his stones and he always found that his ideas would start flowing again. Creative play was also to become a very important aspect of Jungian analysis.

DREAMS, VISIONS AND FANTASIES

Jung found that patients would often report their dreams and fantasies to him spontaneously and he would then ask them questions, e.g. 'Where does that come from?', 'What do *you* think about it?', 'How does it make you feel?' Interpretations of the dreams and fantasies seemed to follow of their own accord from the patients' own replies and associations. Once again, Jung deliberately avoided all theoretical rules – he simply tried to help people to understand their own imagery.

Meanwhile he was also fascinated by his own dreams and he spent a lot of time trying to interpret them, although this was sometimes very difficult. For example, he dreamed of a long row of corpses, each dressed in different clothes going back through the ages to a twelfth-century crusader dressed in chain mail. Each corpse in turn stirred and began to come to life as he looked at it. Jung realized that this particular dream was speaking to him about aspects of the unconscious that are handed down from the ancestors and can still stir and come to life in our own psyches. He felt that the dream tied in with the ideas that he was developing about archetypes and the collective unconscious.

In 1913, Jung began to feel his own immense inner pressure moving outwards, 'as though there were something in the air'. The very atmosphere seemed darker, as if his inner oppression was becoming a concrete reality. During a journey he had an overpowering vision of a huge flood that rose up and covered the whole of northern Europe. The mountains rose higher to protect Switzerland, but all around he saw the rubble of civilization and drowned bodies in a vast sea that turned to blood. The whole vision lasted an hour and made him feel quite ill. Two weeks later it returned, with even more intensity.

This gruesome experience was followed by a recurring dream that began in the spring of 1914. In his dream Jung saw the land frozen to ice in summer time. World War I broke out in August, and Jung knew then that he had to try to understand how his own inner experiences had coincided with the outer experiences of mankind. He realized that the only way to approach this question was to begin to carefully record and study his own fantasies and dreams. He began by writing down ideas that came to him in the course of his creative play. A huge stream of fantasies began to be released and Jung felt that he 'stood helpless before an alien world'. This was hard to cope with, and he felt as if he was enduring an endless series of inner thunderstorms. He knew that he was strong, however, and that he had to find meaning in it all, not only for his own sake, but also for his patients, so that he might better understand their problems. He went on struggling and writing everything down, often having to resort to yoga exercises to try and control his over-wrought emotions.

ARCHETYPES

Jung found that as he wrote he was often using 'high-flown language'. He found this pomposity rather embarrassing, and often felt strong resistance to his fantasies, but he tried to treat the whole thing as a sort of scientific experiment. He knew all too well the dangers of becoming prey to his own fantasies, and how easy it would be to slide into psychosis. Frequently he imagined himself going down a steep descent, until he reached levels as deep as 300 m. After that he felt himself in a cosmic abyss of empty space. He felt as if he was entering the land of the dead and there he began to encounter strange beings.

In one vision he met two figures: a beautiful young girl, accompanied by an old man with a beard. These figures were examples of what Jung called **archetypes**, which form the basic content of religion, myth, art and legend. They are part of the collective unconscious and they emerge in the individual psyche through dreams and visions. Encounters with archetypal figures are often accompanied by a feeling

KEYWORD

Archetype: a recurring image or pattern of thinking which represents a typical human experience.

of a numinous presence and the language they use is often the 'high-flown' language that Jung referred to.

Jung felt that the old man in his vision corresponded to Elijah, an Old Testament prophet, and the young girl to Salome, the archetypal seductress found in the New Testament. Years later he came to realize that this odd couple often appeared in myths. Jung's Elijah character is the wise old prophet, who represents intellect and know-ledge, while Salome represents the erotic element. In Jung's vision they were also accompanied by a large black snake, which Jung explains is a frequent counterpart to the mythic hero.

After a while Jung discovered another arche-typal figure who seemed to evolve out of the Elijah figure. This was Philemon, a pagan sage with **Gnostic** ideas. He first appeared to Jung in a dream, as an old man flying out of a blue sky with clods of earth floating in it. He had the

> **KEYWORD**
>
> Gnostic: relating to knowl-edge, especially occult mystical knowledge.

horns of a bull and the wings of a kingfisher. He carried a bunch of four keys, one of which he held as if ready to open a lock. Jung painted a picture of this apparition and shortly afterwards found a dead kingfisher in his garden by the lakeshore. This was most odd, as kingfishers were rare in the area. Jung saw the incident as providing a crucial insight that there are things in the psyche that we do not produce – they produce themselves and have their own life. He began to have lengthy conversations with Philemon and even went for walks with him in the garden. Philemon explained to Jung that we do not generate our own thoughts – they have an external reality of their own, just like birds in the air, or people in a room.

Jung commented that it was Philemon who taught him 'psychic objectivity, the reality of the psyche'. He realized that there was something within him that could talk about matters that he did not consciously know about, and might even act against him. Archetypal encounters were very important because they enabled Jung to give a personal form

Our thoughts have an external reality of their own.

to aspects of his unconscious. Because they were in some way 'separate' from himself he was able to bring them into relationship with his conscious mind and not get too bogged down in some of their more disturbing utterances. Philemon became an important guru to Jung – psychologically he seemed to have superior insight. Years later Jung met a cultivated Indian who was a friend of Ghandi. He was pleased when he found that this man had no problem with the idea of a spirit guru, and indeed said that many people have them.

In 1916, Jung decided that he wanted to give concrete form to the ideas and insights that had come from Philemon. A restless, ominous atmosphere was beginning to gather in his home. The children had started seeing white figures at night, and had even had their blankets snatched away from them in bed. The doorbell rang frantically by itself when there was nobody there, and the whole house felt thick with spirits. Eventually, a whole host of them infiltrated the house, saying to Jung, 'We have come back from Jerusalem where we found not what we sought.' At this point he put pen to paper and writing poured out of him for three days. He called this writing *Septem Sermones* ('Seven Sermons'). It was written as if the author were addressing the dead, and it represented an exteriorization of all that had been going on in his turbulent mind. The spirits all vanished from the house after that and the weird haunting was over. Jung suggests that they had in fact been parapsychological phenomena, somehow caused by his own highly charged emotional state.

INDIVIDUATION AND THE SELF

Towards the end of World War I, Jung began to emerge from his great darkness. A major event at this time was his discovery of the **mandala**. The word *mandala* comes from Sanskrit and means 'magic circle'. Mandalas are archetypal symbols, found in many religions and in other aspects of many cultures. A basic mandala is a circle containing a square or other symmetrical figure, but there are many variations. The image may represent the universe itself, or the 'inner universe' – the wholeness of the **self**.

KEYWORDS

Mandala: a symbolic circular figure that represents the universe, or the wholeness of the self.

Self: the archetype of wholeness of the psyche which transcends the ego.

Individuation: conscious realization and fulfilment of the self.

Every morning Jung did a small circular drawing of this type and observed the ways in which they changed from day to day. He found that they helped him to observe his own psychic transformations – the ever-changing state of his inner self.

Mandalas fascinated Jung for many years, and he gradually came to understand that they represented the way in which all paths in the psyche led eventually to a mid-point, which is the core, or essence, of the self. The goal of psychic development is the discovery of the unique self. This process is what Jung called **individuation**, and it is one of the core concepts of analytical psychology. The evolution of the psyche is not linear, but a process of 'circumambulation (walking around) of the self'.

Jung used the mandala to explore his ever-changing inner self.

Jung found that his mandala drawings linked up with external experiences in his everyday life and also with his dreams. For example, he drew two mandalas that seemed to be related to one another. The first was inspired by a dream where he was in Liverpool amid rain and fog. Suddenly he came upon an island with a magnolia tree in full blossom upon it. This dream felt very important – Liverpool was the 'pool of life'. When he painted this mandala he felt it was in some way Chinese. Later he did another mandala with a golden castle at the centre of it.

Soon after this, Jung received a letter containing a manuscript of a 1,000-year-old Taoist alchemical writing from China. It was called *The Secret of the Golden Flower*. He related the symbol of the golden flower to the golden castle he had drawn, and the beautiful magnolia tree he had dreamed of. In both cases the circular pattern with the goal in the centre somehow expressed for him the totality of the individual, in both conscious and unconscious aspects. In Eastern religions the mandala is often used in a similar way, as a centring device to help with meditation exercises. From Jung's mandala work emerged his first inklings of his own personal myth, his all-important 'story' that expressed his real being.

THE TOWER AT BOLLINGEN

Jung felt that he was able to gradually put his dreams and fantasies onto a more solid footing and began to understand the unconscious in more scientific terms. He also wanted to make a representation of his innermost thoughts and knowledge in a more permanent, solid way than simply writing them down on paper. For this purpose of self-expression, and also as a quiet retreat, he built his tower at Bollingen in 1922. He had a special resting room within the tower where only he himself was allowed to go without permission. Here he did paintings on the walls and found that he could truly be himself. He found a great sense of inner peace and spiritual concentration within this special room.

Jung kept on adding to the tower throughout his long life. The new bits all represented different parts of his ever-evolving psyche. He felt that this was an important part of his own individuation process, as if he was being reborn in stone. Life at Bollingen was kept deliberately simple – there was no electricity, and Jung chopped all his own wood, drew water from a well, and cooked all his own food. He enjoyed the sense of silence in the place and living in harmony with nature. All around he carved stones, with inscriptions expressing different insights. The creative play aspect that Jung enjoyed at Bollingen was very important as a means for him to access his unconscious. He discovered that most people found it very difficult to explore and understand their own unconscious.

* * * *SUMMARY* * * *

• Jung had a mid-life crisis that he used in a constructive way to explore his own psyche and develop his ideas about the ways in which the psyche operated.

• Myths were very important to Jung because they were expressions of ideas from the collective unconscious.

• Through listening to his inner thoughts and feelings, Jung discovered the importance of creative play as a way of unlocking the unconscious. He himself used this technique throughout his life whenever he needed to relax or find inspiration.

• He also worked with dreams, visions and fantasies, both his own and those of his patients, finding that these often gave insight into the person's inner world.

• Archetypal encounters were important to Jung because they helped him to personify aspects of his unconscious and so bring them into relationship with his conscious mind.

• The real goal of psychic development is individuation – the discovery of the true self. Jung found that the mandala was an excellent symbol of this process.

4 Exploring the Psyche

When Jung talks about the psyche, he means the whole of the mind or spirit, both conscious and unconscious. He talks about it more as if it were a process than a thing. The individual psyche is always seeking growth and wholeness. It is not to be confused with the self, which is the goal, the centre of the mandala, which the psyche is constantly seeking and moving towards. Conscious attitudes within the psyche are always balanced by unconscious attitudes – if a conscious attitude grows too strong then the unconscious will aways seek to restore equilibrium. The unconscious will express its ideas by means of dreams, spontaneous imagery, slips of the tongue and so on. If the unconscious message is ignored then neurosis or even physical disease may result.

THE PERSONAL UNCONSCIOUS

The concept of the unconscious mind affecting the way we behave was not new – in fact, people had been aware of the idea for centuries. Before Freud, however, the unconscious had been largely overlooked or even ignored altogether. His work had made people more aware of the unconscious and the ways in which it operated in both the adult and the developing child. Freud believed that accessing unconscious, repressed memories was the key to resolving neuroses.

Freud was a convinced mechanist and always tried to be strictly scientific in his approach, whereas Jung never lost his interest in the psychic and paranormal aspects of the human mind. This difference was one of the key factors in the rift between Freud and Jung. Like Freud, Jung was convinced that the unconscious had enormous influence, but he viewed the unconscious in a totally different way. Freud's influence on current thinking had turned the unconscious into what Jung describes in *Man and his Symbols* as a sort of mental rubbish heap, a 'dump for moral refuse'. For Jung the unconscious was much more than that. It contained *all* aspects of human nature, 'light and dark, beautiful and ugly, good and evil, profound and silly'. Jung's great discovery, that led him to a whole new approach to psychology, was that 'just as conscious contents can vanish into the unconscious, new contents, which have never yet been conscious, can arise from it'. In other words, the unconscious was no mere rubbish dump, but was infinitely mysterious and full of the seeds of future events and ideas as well as those from the past. Not only could it look forward as well as back in time, it could also reach beyond its individual boundaries into the world of the collective unconscious.

Freud's hostile attitude towards the paranormal irritated Jung, because he saw it as narrow and limiting in its understanding of the psyche. His own aim was to study the many and varied aspects of both the personal unconscious and the collective unconscious, even though he recognized that this was an enormous task. One night when he was visiting Freud he asked him what he thought about **precognition** and **parapsychology** in general. Freud's reply was terse and dismissive and Jung felt that he had to bite his tongue to conceal his irritation. As he did so, he felt his diaphragm grow very hot and then there was a loud bang in Freud's bookcase right next to them, so that both men jumped up in alarm. Jung announced that this was an example of 'catalytic exteriorization phenomenon' (what we would nowadays probably call **psychokinesis**). Freud scoffed at this idea, but Jung contradicted him and predicted a second loud bang to prove his point. This immediately happened, no doubt leaving Jung feeling smug and Freud aghast.

KEYWORDS

Precognition: knowing something in advance, often by paranormal means.

Parapsychology: the study of paranormal mental phenomena.

Psychokinesis: moving things by mental effort, without using any known natural force.

THE COLLECTIVE UNCONSCIOUS

Jung's interest in the collective unconscious began as a result of his work with psychotic patients and his own mid-life crisis. He discovered that the human mind seemed to produce universally recognizable symbols and imagery, and he eventually coined the word 'archetype' to describe such imagery. The collective unconscious has two main aspects:

* **archetypes** which help to give form to our understanding of unconscious ideas;

* **instincts** which are the innate biological drives that determine our behaviour, e.g. the sex drive, hunger, and aggression.

Both these components belong in the collective unconscious because they exist independently of the individual psyche and contain universally recognized, inherited aspects.

Archetypes

Jung says that archetypes are usually religious in nature, and are accompanied by an atmosphere of the numinous. They are images and have no physical existence in the material world, but this does not mean that they have no separate reality of their own. A good example of an archetype is Jung's spirit guide Philemon, who is an archetypal sage or wise man. People form different archetypal images according to the culture they live in, but the archetype itself remains the same. Everyone is familiar with archetypal figures that tend to appear in myths and fairy stories, for example, the old woman, the trickster, the youth, the fool and so on.

Instincts

Jung reflected that civilization has forced us to separate from our basic instincts, but they have not disappeared altogether. Because they are often repressed, they tend to show themselves indirectly, for example as a neurosis, or as an unaccountable mood. They may also appear in dream images, or manifest as slips of the tongue or memory lapses.

Jung wanted to move away from the idea of separate instincts such as hunger, sex and aggression. He found this approach too concrete and decided that it was more helpful to see the various instincts as being different expressions of a single psychic energy. He called this energy **libido**, comparing the concept to the one in physics, where heat, light and electricity are all different aspects of physical energy. Freud had used the term libido to describe the sexual drive, but Jung stressed that it is important not to pick on one single motivating instinct in this way, any more than the physicist would say that all forces derive from heat alone.

KEYWORDS

Libido: motivating psychic energy.

Ego: the centre of consciousness and the sense of identity.

Shadow: the unconscious part of the personality that contains characteristics which one cannot recognize as one's own.

THE EGO

The **ego** is the centre of consciousness and gives us our sense of who we think we are. It organizes and balances the conscious and unconscious aspects of the psyche, giving it a sense of personal identity and purpose. Jung came to identify his own ego with his analytical (number 1) personality. The ego is not the same as the self, which is the whole personality, the goal of the individuation process. But a strong ego can exert a balancing influence, keeping the conscious and unconscious aspects of the personality in equilibrium. An over-inflated ego on the other hand, will form a dictatorial, intolerant personality. Such an ego can become highly unpleasant, even dangerous, seeing itself as all-important, almost god-like.

THE SHADOW

The **shadow** is an unconscious part of the personality that contains weaknesses and other aspects of personality that a person cannot admit to having. The ego and the shadow work together as a balancing pair. Jung related the shadow to his intuitive (number 2) personality. It is usually the first hidden layer of the personality to be encountered when a person begins psychological analysis. One of the primary tasks of the analyst is to begin to make a person aware of the relationship between the ego and the shadow. When a person has a very weak ego they may be in danger of becoming swamped by images from the shadow, rather as Jung himself was during his mid-life crisis.

The shadow is the dark side of our nature – all that we see as being inferior or uncivilized. It often appears in dreams as a dark, usually negative figure, who is always the same sex as the dreamer. The ego wishes to hide shadow aspects of the personality, but in fact the shadow is not necessarily 'bad', so much as primitive in its outlook. If we face our shadow properly, then it can offer us integration between the conscious and unconscious parts of our psyche.

An over-inflated ego often projects the shadow onto other people. **Projection** is a normal and natural process whereby an unconscious characteristic, a fault, or even a talent of one's own, is seen as belonging to another person or object. When the shadow is projected the ego sees the other person, or people, as being evil and can conveniently deny any negative aspects of itself.

KEYWORDS

Projection: process whereby an unconscious characteristic, a fault, or even a talent of one's own is seen as belonging to another person or object.

Zeitgeist: the spirit of the age.

Jung stresses that the psyche is not confined to the individual. Groups have a collective psyche that forms the spirit of the age, or **Zeitgeist**. This collective psyche readily forms a collective shadow, which can be exceedingly dangerous. For example, in World War II the Nazis formed a collective shadow which they projected onto the Jewish people, whom they then saw as being worthless and evil.

Jung urged mankind to take a look at itself. He sensed dark uncontrolled shadow forces building up in civilized society. Society has a tendency to keep its problem aspects tucked away in separate drawers. These deadly, self-created dangers are often projected onto other nations. Jung gave as an example the perceived threat by the Western nations from the communist countries behind the Iron Curtain. He said that we must recognize that shadow projections are moral problems, which cannot be solved by arms races, or economic competition. We need to look at our own shadow, instead of blaming 'them' all the time.

THE PERSONA

The **persona** (from the same Latin word meaning 'actor's mask') is like a mask that the ego creates in order to hide its true nature from society. It is our public face and may be assumed both deliberately and unconsciously. Whenever we relate to others we put on this

KEYWORD

Persona: the public face that a person assumes when relating to others.

mask. The form of the mask depends upon the expectations and conditioning of society, from parents, teachers, peer groups and so on.

It is necessary for each individual to assume a persona sometimes, in order to function normally within society, because it gives some degree of protection to the vulnerable ego. We need it in order to be able to fit in with a certain culture, or to do a particular job for example. Problems only arise when a person totally identifies with the persona. This means that the person becomes nothing but the role they play. Behaviour becomes rigid, and the person is fearful of ever dropping the mask. Such a personality becomes very confined and liable to develop neuroses. There is a failure to see the broader aspects of life beyond the ego's own tiny role – this situation is spiritually suffocating.

Hiding behind the persona.

Every profession has its own persona, and it is quite easy for people to become totally identified with their professional image and hide behind it all the time. Jung went so far as to say that the persona is in fact a kind of false personality that an individual may ultimately end up believing is real.

ANIMA AND ANIMUS

Jung used the word **anima** to describe the personification of the unconscious feminine aspect of a man's personality. The **animus** is the corresponding masculine aspect of a woman's personality. These unconscious aspects of the personality are seen as being very important in regulating behaviour.

KEYWORDS

Anima: the unconscious feminine side of a man's personality.

Animus: the unconscious masculine side of a woman's personality.

The anima

The anima appears in dreams as archetypal figures, such as the seductress, harlot, or divine female spirit guide. She represents a man's feeling nature, which is fascinating and secretive. Because the anima is composed of feelings she may distort a man's understanding. She is often associated with earth and water imagery, such as caves, fertile soil, waterfalls, or the sea.

Jung first became consciously aware of his own anima when he was analysing his fantasies during his mid-life crisis. He asked himself what he was actually doing, and was startled to hear a woman's voice quite clearly announcing 'it is art'. He felt cross about this, and replied that it was nothing to do with art, but the voice again insisted that it was. This voice was the voice of his anima. At first he found her to be a negative force, and felt somewhat in awe of her, but he carefully wrote down all their conversations.

Jung soon realized that by personifying an archetype in this way he was able to bring it into relationship with his own consciousness. This helps to make the archetype less powerful. Jung found his own anima to be 'full of deep cunning'. He saw her as being like everything that is 'unconscious, dark, equivocal and purposeless in a woman', and also mentioned 'her vanity, frigidity, helplessness and so forth'. He realized that if he had taken what she said at face value then he would have seen his work as being rather unreal, like watching a film, so that he would have felt detached from it. He seemed quite afraid of the potential power of the anima, saying that this kind of thinking could 'utterly destroy a man'.

The anima does have a more positive aspect, however, in that she communicates the images of the unconscious to a man's conscious mind. Jung always questioned his own anima when he felt emotionally disturbed. He found that after a while she would always produce a useful image of some sort and his sense of unrest would vanish. For a man to be in touch with his anima is therefore healing and balancing. The anima is not a specific woman, but an archetype. She contains all the ancestral impressions of what it means to be female. Her form will depend very much upon a man's individual knowledge of women. Passionate attractions occur when the anima is projected onto an actual woman, so that the man falls in love. If on the other hand the man over-identifies with the anima, he may become moody, resentful, or effeminate. If a man's anima is very weak then he will find relationships with women difficult.

The animus

Jung does not say as much about the corresponding animus in women, probably because he had no direct experience of it in his own psyche. The animus represents the thinking, logical part of the woman's psyche and he can lead her towards knowledge and true meaning. It is made up of spontaneous, unpremeditated opinions, which can affect a woman's emotional life. The animus appears in dreams as heroes, poets, gurus and so on. He is also represented in imagery of the air and fire elements, such as swords or burning flames. Projection of the animus onto a real man results in the woman falling in love. The animus likes to project himself onto sporting heroes, intellectuals and so on.

Projection of the animus results in a woman falling in love.

If a woman over-identifies with the animus, she becomes dominating, opinionated and pig-headed. The woman's animus development is important in the way she relates to men – if it is weak then she will have problems.

Ideas about the archetypal male or female, from myths, dreams and fantasies, can lead people to have distorted ideas about the opposite sex. For example, the little girl who has been raised on 'Sleeping Beauty' type stories might constantly seek a handsome prince. Jung believed that men were naturally polygamous, and that the anima compensated for this by always appearing as a single woman or female image. Women on the other hand were naturally monogamous, so that the animus often appears as whole groups of men. If it functions properly the anima or animus should act like a sort of bridge or door between the personal unconscious and collective unconscious. In a similar way, the persona acts as a bridge between the ego and the external world.

PROJECTION

Projection is a normal and natural process, and can be positive or negative. It is always accompanied by a strong emotional reaction to a person, object or situation. Obvious examples are falling in love (anima or animus projection), or taking an excessive dislike to someone or something. Projection is an indication that unconscious ideas are trying to break through into the conscious mind. It is not really the other person or thing that we love or loathe, but a part of our own psyche that is projected onto them. It is important here to distinguish between the idea of 'falling in love', which can be likened to having a crush on someone, and the more stable type of love that develops with maturity.

A good example of projection, which also shows how it inevitably tends to break down eventually, is shown by Jung's self-confessed 'crush' on Freud. We could say that Jung was projecting a 'father archetype' onto Freud. Whenever projection like this occurs, it is very difficult to behave rationally and objectively and so the situation tends to lead to conflict. Jung found that, on the one hand, he tended to hang upon Freud's every word, seeing him as a sort of guru. On the other hand, he felt a nagging resistance to his teachings and gradually became highly critical of him. This divided attitude shows that he was still unaware of the underlying subconscious issues that were involved in the relationship. As the psyche matures it is often able to recognize and own its shadow characteristics and the projection is then withdrawn. When we project, we tend to drink in all the attitudes of the other person, and repress criticisms that are trying to surface from our own psyche. These criticisms often appear in dreams.

✳ ✳ ✳ ✳ *SUMMARY* ✳ ✳ ✳ ✳

- Jung emphasized that it was important to study both the personal unconscious and collective unconscious if we are to understand the human psyche.

- Archetypes are helpful because they give form to ideas from the collective unconscious.

- Jung did not find it helpful to identify separate driving instincts within the psyche, preferring instead to use the term 'libido' to describe a general psychic energy.

- The ego (who we think we are) and the shadow (negative aspects of ourselves that we deny) work together in the psyche as a balancing pair.

- The persona is the mask that we wear in order to relate to other people.

- The male psyche has a balancing female aspect – the anima – and the female psyche has a corresponding male aspect – the animus.

- Projection occurs when we see an unconscious characteristic of our own in another person or object.

Dreams and Symbols

THE IMPORTANCE OF DREAMS

Dreams were enormously important to Jung throughout his life, and they are one of the key aspects of Jungian analysis. For Jung, dreams, archetypes and other mental imagery had a separate psychic reality of their own. Jung suggests various different functions that dreams serve:

* to act as compensation for areas of the conscious mind that are deficient or distorted in some way;

* to bring back archetypal memories from the collective unconscious;

* to draw attention to both inner and outer aspects of our lives of which we are not consciously aware.

Freud saw dreams as important for triggering off the free association process. He would pick out a particular symbol and see where the associated train of thought led. Jung felt that this approach was rather limited for several reasons:

* it debases the rich symbolism and imagery contained in many dreams;

* it often leads one off on another path entirely, away from the original meaning of the dream;

* the dream expresses something that the unconscious is trying to convey, therefore it is more important to look at the actual content of the dream.

Jung agreed with Freud when he said that dreams often arose from emotional upsets, in which complexes were also frequently involved. These complexes were like tender spots in the psyche that easily reacted to external stimulus or disturbance. However, Jung pointed out that complexes can also be explored by means of **word association** tests,

KEYWORD

Word association: process where a patient is given a word and then tells the analysts all the ideas that spontaneously come to mind.

contemplation, or conversation – they do not have to wait to be uncovered by a dream.

Jung felt that a dream always had an underlying idea or intention – it is expressing something important that the unconscious wants to say. The intention of the dream can act as a key to helping a person with their individuation process. This is why Jung felt it was important to concentrate on the actual content of the dream, rather than spinning off on a tangent. Once again, Jung is urging that we listen to what the individual patient or dream has to say. To know and understand a person's whole personality and psychic reality it is vital to realize that dreams and symbolic imagery have a very important role to play. Jung saw this insight as a turning point in his psychology.

Jung also began to understand that just as the human embryo develops through the stages of its evolutionary history, so the mind also travels on its own evolutionary journey. Dreams allow recall of past memories, right back into childhood and beyond, to the most primitive instincts from the collective unconscious. As Freud had already recognized, such recall can be very healing in some cases, filling in gaps in memory from infancy and bringing balance or enrichment to the adult psyche. The further a person goes into analysis, the more complex and symbolic their dreams tend to get. They begin to extend beyond personal life and its experiences, into the realm of the collective and mythological.

SYMBOLS

Jung was particularly interested in symbolism that appeared in dreams. The strange mythological fragments that appeared in his own dreams and fantasies and those of his patients were rich in archetypal symbolism. He found that they were often highly numinous in character and therefore felt that they were very important for the growth of the psyche.

A symbol is a term, a name or an image that contains specific associations in addition to its obvious everyday meaning. For example, a rainbow can be a symbol for joy and hope of goods things to come. A symbol differs from a sign in that a sign is always less than the concept that it represents, whereas a symbol stands for something more than its obvious meaning. Symbols often occur spontaneously in dreams and also crop up as symbolic thoughts, acts and even situations. Dreams are not invented consciously – they occur spontaneously and are our main source of knowledge about symbolism. Sometimes inanimate objects are involved in symbolic events – for example, the clock that symbolically stops when someone dies.

Many symbols are not just meaningful for the individual, but are collective. These are often religious symbols, such as the ox, lion, man and eagle that represent the four evangelists in the Christian religion. Animals often crop up

KEYWORD

Primeval: ancient or primitive.

as religious symbols. In Egyptian mythology, for example, the gods are represented as having attributes of animals such as the jackal, hawk and cat. This type of symbolism is used to express ideas that are beyond words. The origin of typical religious symbols is often attributed to the gods themselves, but Jung says that they actually arise from spontaneous **primeval** dreams and fantasies.

A good deal of our perception of reality goes on at a subconscious level, because we are so bombarded with stimuli all the time that we could not possibly register them all. We perceive many more events than we registered consciously. Sometimes these events well up from the subconscious later on – perhaps in a moment of intuition or in a dream. We then realize that they hold emotional meaning or other significance. Jung says that dream symbols are mostly manifestations of the area of the psyche that lies beyond the control of the conscious mind. He likens the way in which the psyche spontaneously produces symbols to the way in which a plant produces a flower. Dreams are therefore seen as evidence of psychic activity and growth.

THE ORIGINS OF DREAMS

There can be many different causes for dreams, and in much of his work Jung discusses many different aspects of the question of their origin. Some of these are as follows.

* **Physical causes**: such as having eaten a huge meal before going to bed.

* **Memory recall**: this may be from the distant past, or just mulling over events from the previous day.

* **Compensations**: for things that one lacks in waking life. Such a dream may highlight a hidden wish or conflict. Recurring dreams are often attempts to compensate for particular defects in the dreamer's attitude to life. This may date from childhood.

* **Looking ahead**: this includes warning dreams and those where we worry about forthcoming events, as well as the more mysterious precognitive dream. Crises in our lives often have a long unconscious history before they actually happen. Recurring dreams may also fall into this category.

* **Oracular dreams**: these are dreams that feel numinous and highly significant to the dreamer – the sort of dream that our ancestors would have interpreted as messages from the gods. They are sometimes precognitive.

ARCHETYPES IN DREAMS

Jung stressed that it is important to understand the individual in the context of mankind's psychic history as well as within his or her own life experience. This means that the analyst needs to have a good grasp of mythology as well as experience with personal dreams. Archetypal images and figures that appear in dreams are not the archetype itself – they are simply representations of it. For example, a dream of the Virgin Mary might be one way of representing the divine mother archetype. Jung exlains that archetypes are closely connected to instincts. Instincts, he says, are physiological urges, which can be percieved by the normal senses, but can also manifest as symbolic images – these are the archetypes.

Archetypes sometimes appear in children's dreams, like Jung's own phallus dream. In *Man and his Symbols* he gives an example of a whole series of dreams recorded and drawn by a ten-year-old girl. The archetypal content is very strong, including an evil snake-like monster that comes and eats all the other animals, and a drunken woman who falls into water and emerges renewed and sober. So far as Jung was able to discover, these images were not related to any mythological ideas or religious beliefs that her family held.

ANALYSING DREAMS

For Jung, the dream story was not like a conscious story, with a logical beginning, middle and end. It was a complex intuitive structure, which must be viewed as a whole, rather than by being picked apart. He also felt that it was important to look at the actual imagery in the individual dream. Each image needs to be considered in turn, always looking at it within the context of the dreamer's own life. For example, supposing someone dreams that they are using a stick to beat down a door. For Freud this would be an obvious sexual symbol, with the stick representing a phallus. Jung pointed out that it could mean something else entirely. The unconscious has deliberately chosen this particular symbol – the analyst's task is to find out why.

Even common dream themes, such as falling, flying and so on, must be viewed in terms of the dream itself. Each dream arises from the individual psyche, in answer to specific circumstances and emotions. It is therefore not possible to lay down general rules for dream interpretation and we should be careful never to impose a meaning on somebody else's dream. We can never fully understand another person's dream and so it is vital to keep our own flow of associations in check. In Jungian analysis:

* the dream should always be treated as a fact. We should make no previous assumptions about it;

* the dream is a specific creation from the unconscious that somehow makes sense, even if we cannot immediately see how;

* we should explore the content of the dream thoroughly to try and find out what unconscious message is trying to emerge.

Dreams have a tendency to occur in series, each separate dream conveying an underlying message in a slightly different way. Jung found that, as a rule, a series of dreams was more useful for interpretation than a single dream. This is because important points become clearer with repetition, and mistakes in interpretation are often corrected by analysing a subsequent dream. The dream can be approached in various different ways.

* **Objectively**: the dream is considered in terms of the person's real life in the external world. For example, if you dream that your car has broken down, perhaps the dream is telling you that it is time to take your car in for a service.

* **Subjectively**: the dream is considered in terms of what it represents within the person's own personality. This time the car might represent yourself – perhaps there is a hidden health problem nagging away at your unconscious mind.

* **Collectively**: if the dream contains numinous, archetypal symbols then we can look towards the collective unconscious and mythological interpretations. For example, if a woman dreams about a brave young warrior, this could be her animus bringing her a message about her need to be more assertive.

JUNG'S HOUSE DREAM

Jung gives an example of a dream that he had about a house and uses it to describe some of the possible pitfalls of interpreting another person's dream. In this dream he was exploring a house on various different levels. He began on the first floor, which was furnished in the style of the eighteenth-century. Below this the ground floor was dark and appeared to be furnished in a sixteenth-century style. The lower down he went, the more primitive the house became, and the bottom cellar was Roman. On the floor here was a stone slab which revealed the way down to a cave full of prehistoric bones and skulls.

When Jung analysed this dream he realized that it was a sort of summary of his own life. He grew up in a house that was about two hundred years old, and his parents' attitude was in many ways medieval. The lower levels illustrated his own passionate interest in ancient history and palaeontology. However, when Jung discussed this dream with Freud, Freud became obsessed with the image of the skulls. He kept returning to them over and over again, insisting that Jung try to find a wish in connection with them. Jung soon realized that he was hinting at a hidden death wish.

Jung concluded that this was his dream, about his own private world. This was important, because he came to understand that dream analysis is not a technique that can be learned and applied by following strict rules – it has to be done by means of discussion between two people. The danger is always that the analyst's interpretation might dominate that of the patient. Jung gave up using hypnosis for the same reason.

Sometimes a dream or vision cannot be understood, however much one tries to investigate it. Jung says that in this case it is best then to leave it at the back of the mind, because it may become clearer at a later date. Often an external event will clarify a dream that one has been mulling over. Jung says that if one carries a dream around for long enough some sense will always emerge from it.

For Jung, dreams and symbols are never pointless nor meaningless. On the other hand they are often not directly connected with worldly concerns, which is why many people tend to dismiss them as being unimportant. Jung says that to him it is incredible that, although we get messages from our unconscious psyche almost every night, most people cannot be bothered to explore their meaning, and often even mistrust or despise them. He wonders in fact, what the unconscious thinks of us! Jung was never able to agree with Freud that a dream was merely a façade, behind which lurked a meaning that was already known but was being withheld from consciousness. Dreams for Jung are often difficult to understand because they are expressed in symbols and pictures, which form the language of the unconscious. They are not deliberately deceptive – they are simply natural attempts by the unconscious to express ideas in its own way.

✳ ✳ ✳ ✳*SUMMARY* ✳ ✳ ✳ ✳

• Dreams were very important to Jung throughout his life and took a central place in his new psychology.

• A dream is personal to the individual and can help with the individuation process. Interpretation should be carried out by means of talking to the dreamer about the actual dream itself.

• The dream can arise from many different sources but it always has a meaning that is relevant to the dreamer.

• The analyst needs to have a good grasp of mythological ideas so that dreams can be looked at in a collective context when archetypal material emerges.

The Personality and Relationships

6

Jung was interested in the conscious aspects of the mind as well as the unconscious. He developed a theory about different types of human personalities that he called his 'psychology of consciousness'. Jung observed that human behaviour tends to follow certain basic patterns, which often operate as pairs of opposites. During the course of development one of each pair often comes to be preferred, so that the person tends to develop that mode of behaviour and act according to its characteristic aspects. The preferred mode of behaviour gradually becomes habitual and leads to predictable personality traits and ways of behaving.

INTROVERSION AND EXTRAVERSION

Jung's theory divided people into two basic types according to the orientation of their psychic energy. The two different attitudes were called **introversion** and **extraversion**, and the two psychological types 'introverts' and 'extraverts'. These terms are so well-known today that people take them for granted in everyday use of language. Everyone has both attitudes to varying degrees, but there is a tendency for one of them to dominate.

KEYWORDS

Introversion: direction of interest inwards towards the inner world of thoughts and feelings.

Extraversion: direction of interest outwards towards external objects and relationships.

✳ **Introverts**: withdraw energy from the world and are more interested in their own inner world than the external world. Their behaviour is governed mainly by subjective factors. They are reflective, hesitant people, with retiring natures, preferring to keep themselves to themselves. They are cautious, often shrinking away from new objects and situations and may appear to be somewhat defensive. Introverts need privacy and personal space.

✳ **Extraverts**: direct their energy outwards towards the world. They are interested in external things and relationships and their behaviour tends to be governed by **objective factors**. They are outgoing and frank, with accommodating, adaptable personalities. Extraverts need action and other people around them.

Usually one or other attitude will dominate in the personality and the opposite attitude becomes unconscious. The psyche will then tend to find compensatory ways of expressing this hidden attitude. The two types of attitude tend to clash because where the extravert will follow the crowd, the introvert will deliberately reject the majority view. The introvert likes peace and solitude, whereas the extravert likes to be active and sociable.

Jung realized that nobody ever fitted exactly into one type. People have an infinite variety of different personalities and it would be too narrow and simplistic to fit them neatly into two categories. Because we all possess both attitudes, it is more a question of whether one predominates over the other. Jung's theory is not really an attempt to explain *individual* psychology – it is a generalization, aimed at trying to explain human behaviour. He developed his theory about personality further, to include four 'functions' in addition to the two attitudes.

THE FOUR FUNCTIONS

The idea of there being four balanced elements within nature is very old. **Shamanic** and magical traditions often use a system where the four elements – earth, air, fire and water – are related to the four directions – north, east, south and west. Each element is also associated with different corresponding energies that are represented symbolically by animals, plants, seasons, colours and so on. For example, south is usually associated with the fire element, so an appropriate animal might be a dragon, the colour could be red and the season summer.

Long ago in Ancient Greece, doctors and philosophers began to identify four personality types, based on the same idea of four balanced natural energies. These types, or 'humours', were called: melancholic; sanguine; choleric; phlegmatic. Jung developed a theory of four personality functions based on a similar idea. His **four functions** are grouped as two opposite pairs, giving them a feeling of balance. He named the four functions: *thinking; feeling; sensation; intuition.*

The four functions.

Thinking and feeling are classed as rational functions, because they rely upon internal, mental processes. They determine the way in which a person judges and evaluates experiences. Sensation and intuition are classed as irrational functions because they rely upon objective stimuli. They determine the way in which a person perceives experiences.

Thinking

This tells you what something is. Thinking people have logical, probing and questioning minds. They are good at seeing cause and effect, judging things and reaching logical conclusions by using their intellect. They are frank and may appear cool and distant emotionally. This type is good at adapting to new circumstances.

Feeling

This tells you whether something is agreeable to you or not. Feeling people make judgements about how they value things. Jung stresses that 'feeling' is not used here in the emotional sense – that would imply irrational thinking. Jung is referring here to a rational function, used for putting things in order of value. Feeling people have a strong sense of traditional values and human relationships are important to them. They are often warm, creative people.

Sensation

This tells you that something exists. This type of person relies very much upon actual sensory impressions. They assess their world by how things look, what words sound like and so on. Material things are very important to them and they are solid, grounded people. They take everything at face value and 'call a spade a spade'. They can be boring and plodding, lacking in imagination, but on the other hand they are happy and easygoing. Their calm nature makes them appear rational and logical, but this is not always the case.

Intuition

This gives you hunches about things. This type of person is aware of chances, possibilities, the past and the future. They are often not aware of their own bodies and may be dreamy and ungrounded. They can become impatient with solid, monotonous detail and they are not practical people. Intuitive people are able to perceive possibilities that are not known consciously through the normal senses.

A person's conscious orientation will usually be towards one of the four functions. This dominant function will determine how the person reacts to experiences. Its opposite function remains largely unconscious and the two left over functions are partially conscious, partially unconscious. When the conscious function is particularly strong there is a tendency for the opposite function to break through into consciousness now and again. This is called 'the return of the repressed' and it may manifest as hysteria, phobias, obsessions, unbalanced moods and so on. In order to gain a balanced, healthy mental attitude it is often necessary to work with the repressed function in therapy.

THE EIGHT PSYCHOLOGICAL TYPES

Each of the four functional types of personality may be extraverted or introverted. Jung therefore combined the four functions and the two attitudes, to arrive at **eight psychological types**. A person's psychological type is important in determining their view of the world and how they cope with situations and relationships.

KEYWORD

Eight psychological types: combinations of the four personality types and the two attitudes (introversion and extroversion).

The extravert thinking type

This type is dominated by rational thinking and logic. They love order and facts, and tend to think that their view of the world is the correct one. They have a tendency to become tyrants. In actual fact, they conveniently suppress anything that doesn't fit in with their world view. What they repress may return as violent moods, wild love affairs and so on. They have a strong sense of duty, but they may lack warmth and tolerance. Many scientists and engineers may belong to this type.

The introvert thinking type

This type is more interested in the inner world of ideas than external facts. They constantly ask questions and formulate theories about things, but they are reserved about accepting 'facts'. They may appear eccentric to others, and may be so cut off from the world that relationships are unimportant to them. Philosophers and professors may belong to this type.

The extravert feeling type

This type is well-adjusted to the world around them and fits in well with their peer group. They are conventional, concerned with personal success. They are tactful and charming, handling people well, and enjoy social gatherings and groups. On the negative side they can be rather shallow and insincere. Good hostesses and people in social work may belong to this group.

The introvert feeling type

This type is rather remote and inward-looking – the 'still waters run deep' type of person. They are reserved and enjoy peace and quiet, poetry and music. They prefer to have a few intimate friends and actually understand people who are close to them pretty well. They are often very religious and self-sacrificing. These people are usually genuine, because they are hopeless at role-playing, and they make loyal friends. Monks and nuns may belong to this group.

The extravert sensation type

For this type, objects and sensations in the outside world are very important. This is the practical, man-of-the-world type who accepts the world as it is and enjoys living in it. The down side is that they can be addictive and pleasure-seeking and extreme cases have a tendency towards perversion. People of this type are often in business or property dealing.

The introvert sensation type

With this type it is the internal, subjectively experienced sensation that is important. Objects do not count much. They are so full of their own sensations that they may appear out of touch and find it hard to express themselves to others. They may claim to see ghosts, visions and star-tling imagery. Some artists and musicians may belong to this group.

The extravert intuitive type

This type uses the intuitive part of the brain whenever a judgement or decision has to be made without knowing the full facts. They get bored with fixed, familiar, well-established things and like to explore the new and look to the future. Because of this they may view customs and conventions as unimportant, and may trample on other people in order to get what they want. They are 'chancers', with their own form of morality. They rarely see a thing through to the end and their personal relationships are weak. Entrepreneurs and businessmen may belong to this group.

The introvert intuitive type

To this type, the mystical world of dreams, visions and the collective unconscious is important. They are often pre-occupied with inner day-dreams, fantasies and religious revelations. In the past, this type of person would have probably been the shaman of the tribe, but nowadays they are often outcast and regarded as being 'odd'. Many psychics, mystics and poets belong in this group.

FORMING RELATIONSHIPS

It is of course rare, if not impossible, to find a person who represents a pure type. The types are really intended to represent general behavioural tendencies, rather than concrete personality categories. Most people are a mixture of at least two types and more complex personalities probably incorporate more. Gaining insight into a person's psychological type can assist progress in therapy, or help to understand a relationship. People may gradually change their type as they develop and mature. Integration of the different types within the personality can be seen as the goal of the individuation process. The more mature the psyche becomes, the more a person is consciously aware of different aspects of the self.

People are often attracted to their opposite type because their partner expresses the neglected function. There are two dangers here:

* people may avoid achieving their own psychological wholeness because they see their neglected function as belonging to the other person;

* because opposite types do not understand each other many misunderstanding can arise.

When a person projects their own hidden aspect onto someone else they 'fall in love' with them. As they become more aware of their own unconscious aspect this projection tends to be withdrawn and they fall out of love again.

Sometimes people fall for the same type as themselves. This means that the dominant function tends to get over-emphasized and the suppressed one causes all sorts of havoc in the relationship. For example, two introverted, intuitive poets might get together and live in a fantasy world, totally neglecting their surroundings and living in squalor.

Two introverted intuitive poets living together.

THE DEVELOPING PSYCHE

A person's psychological type begins to become apparent quite early in childhood. It is determined by a number of different factors.

* **Heredity:** genetic factors will tend to predispose a child to being more introverted or extraverted.

* **Parental type:** the child may identify with one or other parent and so begin to copy their behaviour. Alternatively they may deliberately develop an opposite type in order to rebel.

* **Social factors:** whichever behaviour is encouraged and achieves the best results will also influence the development of a psychological type. The family, school, peer group and so on are all important here. Extravert children soon appear to be more active, talkative, sociable and interested in their surroundings. This type of outlook is favoured in modern western society and so it will tend to be encouraged.

Problems often arise when parents try to force a child into a mould that goes against the natural type. This sort of pressure can result in neurosis and hampers development in later life. If the parents are more flexible they can help the child towards individuation. Often the unconscious function is projected onto others as the child grows – perhaps onto parents, siblings, peer group members, actors or pop stars. The child will identify with groups or fall in love with people who satisfy this function. Through a process of repeated projection and subsequent withdrawal the whole psyche gradually becomes more integrated. This is why attachments of this sort are so important to the developing psyche.

Emotional involvement frequently occurs between patient and analyst during the course of therapy. This process is actually a kind of projection and is called **transference**. It can work in either direction and may be positive or negative in nature. It can be useful if it is handled

KEYWORD

Transference: emotional involvement between patient and therapist.

sensitively, because once the feelings are projected onto the other person it becomes possible to draw them out and look at them objectively.

The development of the psyche is never static and complete, but always growing and changing. Psychological changes, directed from within may continue throughout adult life if a person is willing to grow. Jung says that the second half of life should have a very different quality form the first half. He compares the journey of the psyche to the daily journey of the sun, rising towards the zenith and then falling again. In the first half of life we are concerned with achievement, establishing ourselves in the world, earning a living, raising a family and so on. The problems we encounter are mainly biological and social. Later in life we can become more inward-looking and reflective. The problems we are involved with become more cultural and spiritual in nature. Confronting and integrating the repressed aspects of the personality may now lead eventually to the individuation of the psyche.

*** ***SUMMARY*** ***

• Jung idenitified two opposite and balanced attitudes – introversion and extraversion – which characterized human psychological make-up.

• He then established four different functions – thinking, feeling, sensation and intuition – which he grouped into two opposite and balanced pairs.

• The two attitudes and the four functions were then combined to produce eight different psychological types.

• A person's psychological type will influence their relationships and the way they function in the world. Most people are a mixture of two or more types.

• A person's psychological type can change and mature throughout their life. More integrated people are more consciously aware of all the different functions within their personality.

The Esoteric and the Paranormal

Jung did not see human beings as purely biological organisms in the way that Freud had tended to, nor was he interested only in treating neurosis and mental illness. For him, the spiritual aspects of the psyche were both fascinating and vitally important. In fact, he saw the numinous aspects of human psychology as holding the true key to therapy.

Throughout his long life, Jung had a fascination with exploring the **esoteric** and the paranormal and he wrote an enormous amount about subjects relating to both areas. His range of interests, was vast, and this approach was quite deliberate, because he was searching for universal truths within human psychology that would link up with his theories about the collective unconscious. This huge diversity of interests make it very difficult to decide who Jung really was – he was almost certainly a genius, but reactions to his work vary between those who see him as a sort of guru or mystic, and those who slate him as a charlatan. His interest in the **occult** has made him open to the latter criticism.

GNOSTICISM

Gnosticism is a religious and philosophical movement, which probably originated in around the fourth century BC. There were many different Gnostic sects, all concerned with knowledge of the occult and the magical. In fact *gnosis* is derived from a Greek word, meaning 'knowledge'.

Jung studied Gnosticism in depth from about 1918 until 1926. His interest first arose because he was keen to establish historical and literary links with his ideas about human psychology. He saw his analytical psychology as being fundamentally a natural science, but he was well aware that it was all too easy to introduce personal bias to his findings.

He needed some kind of credibility and he thought that this might be achieved if he could demonstrate parallels between his own thinking and that of the Gnostics.

Jung discovered that mythological ideas within Gnosticism had great relevance to his ideas about the human psyche. In Gnostic thinking, nature and creation are fundamentally flawed and separated from the original true god. The world is ruled over by its creator, who is not really the original god, but a sort of 'half-god' or 'demi-urge'. He is assisted by seven beings called 'archons', who try to enslave people and prevent their return to the original divine realm. Gnosis was supposed to offer a key to the return to the divine.

Jung saw this myth as being symbolic of the individuation process, where the soul goes on its own inner spiritual quest, seeking inner unity with the self. At the start of the quest it is as blind to its true nature as the Gnostic soul is to the nature of the true god. Jung was excited about this because it seemed to show that his ideas were indeed not new and had indeed been at large throughout history. Eventually, however, he decided that Gnostic teachings were too remote and obscure – they had been formulated a very long time ago, and any knowledge we have of them was mainly recorded by Christians, who were in fact rivals to the Gnostics.

ALCHEMY

When Jung first began reading about alchemy he found it far-fetched and difficult to understand. However, after reading *The Secret of the Golden Flower*, the book of Chinese alchemy that linked up with his own dreams (see Chapter 3), he became seriously interested in the subject, and was eventually to be profoundly affected by the insights of alchemy.

> **KEYWORD**
>
> Alchemy: an esoteric practice combining aspects of mysticism, magic, science and religion.

Alchemy was very popular during medieval times, but its roots stretch back much further into history. The best-known aspect of alchemy is the idea of trying to turn base metals into gold, but in fact there was more to it than that. The ultimate goal was an inner transformation of the alchemist's psyche, and it was this aspect that interested Jung the most. He saw alchemy as bridging the frustrating gap between ancient Gnosticism and modern sciences such as chemistry and the psychology of the unconscious. Alchemical thought coincided in surprising ways with his own ideas about the unconscious, so that Jung saw alchemy as the historical counterpart of his analytical psychology that he had been looking for. This gave more substance to his ideas.

Alchemy is full of weird fantasy images, which Jung soon realized were archetypal in nature. This was important because he realized that understanding historical ideas could be vital in understanding the psychology of the unconscious. The idea of turning base metal into gold was rooted in still earlier ideas about the four elements – earth, air, fire and water. Every physical form was supposed to contain these four elements in different proportions. Alchemists believed that if one could somehow alter the balance, then bingo – base metal into gold! Success depended very much upon the alchemist's state of mind, which naturally had to be pure, and prayer and meditation were part of the practice.

The alchemist's state of mind naturally had to be pure.

Jung was intrigued to find alchemical imagery cropping up in the dreams of patients who were going through the individuation process. He studied the alchemical process and found that it went through a series of stages, each one of which could also represent a stage in the development of the maturing psyche.

* **Nigredo or 'blackness':** This the first stage, when the alchemist heats stuff up until it goes black. This represents the first stage of individuation, where the person begins to break down the barriers between conscious and unconscious. This stage is often accompanied by depression – the 'dark night of the soul', as the person begins to face the inner darkness of the shadow.

* **Albedo or 'whiteness':** This is the next stage, when white flecks appear in the mixture, which eventually crystallize as a white stone. This represents the gradual cleansing of the psyche as the inner darkness is faced. People often confront and converse with archetypes at this stage, and interestingly the alchemists reported meeting all kinds of frightening mythical beings wondering around their labs.

* **Rubedo or 'redness':** This is the final stage, when mercury is added to the white stone, which goes green, then red. This process represents the union of opposites and the result – which is called *elixir vitae* (the elixir of life) – can bring long life or even immortality. It is represented symbolically by a winged hermaphrodite figure, or a rose. This stage represents the final stage of analysis – the resolution of psychic conflicts and the balancing of opposites. Jung remarked that much of his work was concerned with this type of balancing process.

THE I CHING

Jung's early interest in omens and paranormal occurrences led him towards an exploration of various types of **divination**. He developed a special interest in the **I Ching**, an ancient Chinese method of divination. The I Ching is also known as the *Book of Changes* and this gives a clue to the philosophy behind it. From ancient times the Chinese have seen creation as being made up of intertwined male and female energies, each carrying the seed of the other. This is represented by the well known black-and-white **yin and yang** symbol.

The universe is in a constant state of change as the two primal forces flow in and out of each other. This idea of wholeness and the balancing of two opposite forces fits in very well with Jung's ideas, and the yin and yang symbol is another example of the archetypal mandala. To consult the I Ching, yarrow stalks or coins were usually used. Short and long stalks, or the two sides of a coin, represented the two primal forces. The stalks or coins were thrown and the random patterns they made interpreted by using a special book of wise sayings. Jung, in the peace of his retreat at Bollingen, used reeds in place of yarrow stalks.

KEYWORDS

Divination: insight into the future or the unknown gained by paranormal methods.

I Ching: ancient Chinese method of divination.

Yin and yang: the two balanced and opposite principles that operate in the universe according to Chinese philosophy.

The yin and yang symbol.

Jung was fascinated by the results he obtained from I Ching readings. He found many 'meaningful connections with my own thought processes which I could not explain to myself'. He began to use the I Ching with his patients too, and found that a significant number of the answers given were relevant to the patients' problems. For example, a young client was wondering whether he should marry a certain girl. When the I Ching was consulted it gave the reply: 'The maiden is powerful. One should not marry such a maiden.' The girl seemed suitable, but deep down the young man was afraid that she would soon become like his dominating mother.

Jung began to wonder how such meaningful answers could emerge from the I Ching. How did the connection between the inner, psychic event and the outer, physical event come about? Jung suggested the idea of 'acausal parallelism', by which he meant that two events could be connected in some way, without one necessarily having to be the direct cause of the other. He later used the word **synchronicity** to express this idea.

KEYWORDS

Synchronicity: the simultaneous occurence of two meaningful but not causally connected events.

Causality: the idea that related events are connected by cause and effect.

SYNCHRONICITY

Science has tended to train people to think that A causes B which causes C, in a neat orderly, linear fashion. So related events are connected by cause and effect – this idea is known as **causality**.

Eastern thinking, as Jung discovered by playing with the I Ching, has long taught that there is another way in which events can be connected. A and B are connected, but neither need be the cause of the other. This is what Jung called synchronicity and he suggested that coincidences worked in this way.

Jung wondered if a law of synchronicity could be established, contrasting with the law of causality. He was very excited by the idea of discovering a place where psychology and physics could meet and some scientists, notably Nobel prize winner Wolfgang Pauli (1945, Nobel Laureate in Physics), were interested in Jung's ideas. Modern quantum physics seems happy to accept acausal effects in its physical theories. Physicists have even suggested that physical bodies can sometimes have an effect upon one another without any apparent exchange of energy taking place between them. The universe no longer seems to consist of facts, but of possibilities.

Jung was especially interested in the more startling coincidences, those that seemed to be so meaningful that it was virtually impossible for them to have occurred by chance alone. Simple coincidences, such as reading a new word in the paper and then immediately coming across it in the crossword, did not hold quite such fascination for him.

For example, he was listening one day to a young woman patient who was relating to him a dream about being given a golden scarab. As she spoke he heard a tapping on the window, and upon opening it he found a scarabaeid beetle, the local equivalent of the golden scarab. The woman was so surprised by this event that it changed her whole way of thinking, breaking down her rational defences and leading to new mental maturity. The scarab, as Jung pointed out, is an archetypal symbol of rebirth. Such archetypal symbolism often seems to crop up in connection with synchronous events.

ASTROLOGY

Jung was interested in **astrology** because it too tied up with his ideas about archetypes and the collective unconscious. He did a great deal of careful research, learning how to draw up **natal charts** and finding out how they linked up with events in people's lives. He was fascinated by the idea that a person's private world could be affected by far-reaching aspects of cosmic activity. He was not at all interested in the generalized type of astrology that appears in newspapers and magazines.

KEYWORDS

Astrology: study of the ways in which celestial bodies affect human affairs.

Natal chart: chart showing the position of the celestial bodies at the time of someone's birth.

Jung decided that astrology would be a good way of showing synchronicity at work as a natural law in its own right. He studied the birth charts of married couples, to see if the positions of the planets in the two natal charts tied in with the actual marriage event. If this could be shown to happen then he would have established a meaningful acausal link. He did not find a direct correlation, but what he did find was equally fascinating. He found that the results of analysis varied according to who was doing the actual analysis. In other words, a person's subjective expectations were somehow mirrored in the results. Modern physics is beginning to see this as a real possibility – the observer can affect the results of an experiment simply by the act of observing.

Jung was also interested in the precession of the **equinoxes**. This phrase describes the way in which the astrological sign in which, for example, the spring equinox occurs moves slowly backwards through one degree longitude every 72 years. So in 2000 years the sign

KEYWORD

Equinoxes: days (two a year) on which day and night are of equal length

on the horizon at the time of equinox changes. At the moment we are just leaving the Age of Pisces and entering the Age of Aquarius. Jung believed that this phenomenon had far-reaching effects upon both historical events and human spirituality. Each 2000-year change heralds the beginning of a new spiritual trend. Interestingly, Jesus was born at the beginning of the Age of Pisces, and his sign is often shown as that of the fish. We are now apparently due for a change as we enter the Age of Aquarius....

AS ABOVE SO BELOW

Jung's view of the human psyche in many ways reflected the ancient occult maxim 'as above so below'. For him, events in the outer world of material things were often reflected in the inner world of the psyche. this effect could also take place in reverse, with the individual affecting the surroundings. Jung discovered that as patients got deeper into therapy, synchronous psychic events became more frequent in their lives.

He concluded that a human being is not an isolated psyche, but part of a vast network of interacting energy that can affect us in many unexpected ways. Since psyche and matter are part of the same unfathomable universe and in constant contact with each other, Jung thought it possible, if not probable, that they actually represented two different aspects of a whole.

Jung felt that many personal psychological problems arose from a sort of family or cultural karma – problems that had not been resolved by one's forebears were passed on to be sorted out. He said that many problems are more to do with the social environment than the individual and are therefore linked to the collective unconscious. Jung observed that so far psychological therapy had been slow to take this into account.

Jung's view of the world was often subjective, concentrating on the inner world of dreams, visions and synchoronous events. He saw his life's quest as being one of achieving understanding of his own unconscious and so in many ways the inner world was even more important than the outer world. At times he would deliberately try to shut himself off from the sensory input of the outside world and spend time alone in order to enter his own rich, inner world. If we live too much in the outer world he said, 'we are held to the hour and minute of the present and have no way of knowing how our ancestral psyches listen to and understand the present – in other words, how our unconscious is responding to it'. It is essential to listen to the voice of the unconscious in order to balance the historical psychological aspects of our being with the 'ephemeral conditions of the present'. Through his studies of the esoteric and the paranormal, in the peace and silence of his retreat at Bollingen, Jung was able to achieve this state of being and 'see life in the round'.

* * * *SUMMARY * * * *

● Jung was fascinated by a wide range of esoteric and paranormal studies.

● In these studies he was searching for universal truths within human psychology that would link up with his theories about the collective unconscious.

● In both Gnosticism and alchemy he discovered an archetypal symbolism and mythology that supported his theories.

● His studies of divination and astrology led him to suggest the existence of a second natural law, that of synchronicity that worked alongside the law of causality.

● Jung believed that events in the outer world of material things were often reflected in the inner world of the psyche, and vice-versa.

Religion and Spirituality 8

JUNG'S SPIRITUAL ATTITUDE

Jung was by nature a spiritually aware person, and this was one of the most important aspects of his life. However, he had a tendency to attack the dogma of the great religious faiths, asserting that spontaneous, personal religious experiences led to spiritual truth. In religious matters, as in psychotherapy, it was the individual person's unique life experience that really counted in Jung's view. He maintained that the unconscious is our only source of spiritual experience and that the individual can only attain enlightenment through a process of painstaking self-examination. Jung always tried to approach religious questions from the point of view of a rational scientist and he explored many different religious angles in his search for universal truths.

Jung used Biblical references quite frequently in his writing, and also made references to the Apocrypha, a collection of texts that were included in some versions of the Old Testament, but not in the Hebrew Bible, and that contains writings that have not been accepted by mainstream Christianity. As was the case with his studies of Gnosticism and alchemy, he used these texts as a source of material to support his own analytical psychology. Once again he emphasized the symbolic and mythological aspects which gave archetypal insights and were used to express ideas that could not be expressed directly in ordinary language.

Although Jung was always drawn to discover more about the numinous, his relationship with Christianity was always somewhat ambiguous. He found the conservative dogma and ritual of his father's Christianity too limiting. In fact some of the ideas he found positively distasteful – above all, the idea that God, who had made people imperfect in the first place, could be appeased by the sacrifice of his own son. As he attempted to grow away from his religious upbringing, he developed some ambivalent attitudes. Meanwhile, his mother's views were less rigid and she introduced him to ideas from other religions and encouraged his early interest in the paranormal.

THE PROBLEM OF EVIL

Astrological ideas suggested to Jung that the Age of Pisces had coincided with the birth of Christ and the subsequent growth of Christianity. Jung emphasized that for him the Christian insistence that God the Father and Jesus were sinless beings represented an unbalanced attitude – a total denial of the shadow. Jung predicted an inevitable swing eventually to counteract this trend. He saw this beginning with the nineteenth-century teachings of thinkers such as Marx and Darwin, whose rationalist, materialist stance came into conflict with Christianity. But Jung felt that modern man has gained scientific insight at the cost of losing his soul – he was no longer in contact with the numinous.

A lack of understanding of what goes on in the unconscious is dangerous, because it means that we are afraid to confront the shadow and therefore do not develop the capacity to deal with evil. Jung asserts that none of us is without our darker aspects. It is important in religious matters, as in human relationships, to see and acknowledge our imperfections because 'where love stops, power begins, and violence and terror'. Chilling words.

Jung's attitude to the problem of evil is probably the most important way in which his thinking differs from traditional Christian theology. He struggled during his teens with a great spiritual crisis that led him to the idea that God *must* have a darker side to his nature, otherwise he would never have created the serpent in order to tempt Adam and Eve towards sin. In other words, God must have made the first people with a deliberate capacity for sin.

Jung had a strange vision at this time: 'I saw before me the cathedral, the blue sky. God sits on His golden throne, high above the world – and from under the throne an enormous turd falls upon the sparkling new roof, shatters it, and breaks the walls of the cathedral asunder.'

This vision was followed by an indescribable sense of relief, as Jung realized that what really mattered for him was to follow the will of the living, active God, rather than blindly following handed-down traditions and Biblical texts. From this experience also came the 'dim understanding that God could be something terrible'. For Jung, in fact, God was both 'the annihilating fire and an indescribable grace'. Once again we find the idea of balanced opposites that are so important in Jung's thinking.

THE STORY OF JOB

One of Jung's most controversial books was *Answer to Job*, published near the end of his life in 1952. Jung uses his own interpretation of the Old Testament story of Job to explore his idea of the shadow aspect of God. The story tells of how the devil bets God that Job will turn against him if he is tormented enough. God takes up the devil's bet and sends Job all kinds of nasty trials and tribulations. Jung's fundamental question is: if God is all-good, then where does evil come from, and how does God permit it to exist? Jung suggests that the Old Testament God, who torments Job is unpleasant and frightening and yet he demands love from Job. For Jung this is a demonstration of God's shadow side.

Jung's idea is that God actually goes through an individuation process of his own, gradually becoming more mature and whole. He traces the course of this development through the Bible until we reach the point where God really wants to transform himself through becoming human. Eventually, by being incarnated as Jesus, God fully experiences what he had made Job suffer.

Jung was fascinated by the weird apocalyptic visions in the book of Revelations at the end of the Bible. He suggests that they represent a final confrontation with the shadow, where God gives vent to his anger at the way his creation has turned out. Jung suggests that after the apocalypse a new divine goddess figure will emerge, representing a balancing energy after an era of male dominance and destructiveness. What Jung really seems to be suggesting is the idea that as people's understanding of God evolves, so God himself also evolves.

The notion that God could have a negative, shadow side has perturbed a lot of Christians. But Jung's idea is that we all need to transform the negativity in ourselves before we can hope to transform the outer world. This is what we are trying to do in the search for the self. The self represents a deeper, wiser aspect of our being that knows our life's purpose and our true path.

THE JOURNEY TOWARDS THE SELF

Jung saw Christ as providing people with an archetypal image of the self to which they can aspire. Other religions also have their own figures, such as Buddha, who represents spiritual perfection and wholeness. Just as God sent his son Christ into the world, so each of us sends our ego into the outer world. The goal of the individuation process is the eventual re-integration of the self, whereupon it ceases to occupy centre stage in our consciousness. This is a lengthy and very painful process, which Jung compares with the difficult initiation tests often undergone by members of shamanic tribes. Such tests are often designed to bring initiates to the brink of death after which they emerge with new spiritual awareness. After this the shaman is able to be a healer and spiritual teacher.

Jung identifies this archetypal death and rebirth process occurring in different forms in many cultures and religious traditions, for example in:

* the death and resurrection of Jesus;
* the alchemical process where a base metal is broken down and eventually transmuted into the *Elixir Vitae*;
* shamanic initiation rituals;
* ancient Egyptian myths, where again the god dies and is re-born.

Interestingly, in the Egyptian tradition, rebirth was originally only a possibility for the Pharaoh, who was a god-like being, but eventually it became available to others who followed the correct burial rites. Jung's vision was that eventually a kind of psychic rebirth would be available for everyone who was willing to undergo the individuation process.

Naturally Jung's unorthodox views about religion opened him to criticism from theologians, who resented his trespassing on their territory. He disagreed totally with **fundamentalist** points of view, where people held that their own particular brand of belief represented absolute truth. Jung tended more towards the Gnostic view that it was knowledge that counted, rather than faith. He cautioned that whenever **dogma** takes over human minds, they lose sight of whatever spiritual insights they had in the first place. Jung felt it was necessary for him as a psychologist to explore this important area of the human psyche in as much depth as possible and so he also made in-depth studies of some of the Eastern religions.

> **KEYWORDS**
>
> **Fundamentalist:** strict adherence to ancient doctrines and texts of a religion.
>
> **Dogma:** principle beliefs laid down by religious authorities.
>
> **Yoga:** Hindu system of philosophy involving meditation, physical exercises and other spiritual practices.

HINDUISM

In the Hindu faith, there are many gods and goddesses who all originate from an original creative force called Brahma. Each god and goddess symbolically represents a different divine aspect – such as Vishnu the creator, Shiva the destroyer, or Krishna the god of love. Unlike in the Christian tradition, the shadow side of the divine is openly portrayed.

Jung became interested in **yoga**, which is a Hindu system of philosophy using physical exercises and meditation as a means of attaining ultimate reunion with the divine. He found the familiar physical postures helpful for calming the mind and he was fascinated by the symbolic process of spiritual transformation described in the yogic texts. Once again he found a description of the archetypal process of separation and eventual rebalancing of opposites, just as he had seen it in the alchemical texts.

Jung saw the physical and meditative processes of yoga as a useful means of relaxing the ego's grip over the unconscious, so that the individuation process could get underway. He cautioned Western people not to go too deeply into the more obscure practises of yoga, warning that Western minds are not usually properly prepared and that total psychosis could result.

Although he was impressed by the Hindu religion and yoga, Jung could not accept the ultimate goal, *samadhi*, or the total absorption of the self into the divine. He argued that such a state would be logically impossible, because if there is no self, then there is no consciousness, so who can be experiencing *samadhi*? In any case, he was not at all happy with an ultimate goal that seemed to represent a total escape from reality. This seemed to him to be pointless and he believed instead that each of us is in the world for a special purpose, which is known to the self and which it is our task to discover. The goal of Jungian analysis was to help people towards wholeness and to function more fully in the real world.

BUDDHISM
The goal of Buddhism is to attain an inner state of enlightenment, once again detaching oneself from the physical world and the endless chatter of the psyche. In Zen Buddhism the student studies riddles called *koans*, e.g. 'what is the sound of one hand clapping?' Of course there is no logical answer – the purpose of the *koan* is to demonstrate the futility of trying to achieve enlightenment through logical thinking. Jung saw parallels here with psychological therapy, where the aim is to alter conscious awareness and achieve a higher spiritual state.

Jung was particularly interested in *The Tibetan Book of the Dead* – a sort of travel guide for the departed soul. This tied up with other texts that he had discovered, for example in Ancient Egyptian mythology, where there is also a *Book of the Dead*. He had explored similar themes when he wrote the *Septeme Sermons* (1916) and once again he was struck by the archetypal nature of the teachings that he found cropping up in different cultures. In other Buddhist teachings, he found vivid archetypal imagery, such as the 'jewel in the crown of the lotus', which he saw as another mandala-like symbolic image for the self.

Buddhism appealed to Jung because:

* it is up to each person to follow his or her own path to enlightenment – there is little emphasis upon dogma and faith;

* the answer to spiritual growth is seen as lying within – there is no external deity as such;

* the spiritual teachings and meditations are helpful for training the mind towards concentration.

Nevertheless, he also found that there were drawbacks. In Buddhism, suffering is seen as an illusion from which one can ultimately escape through attaining enlightenment. Jung disagreed, saying that suffering is real and unavoidable. We can only overcome suffering by living through it and analytical psychology can help us to do that. Also, withdrawal from life is in itself a form of repression – a denial of the shadow – and as such would tend to produce an opposite swing eventually.

Finally, in Buddhism there is an endless cycle of reincarnation, where the individual is born and dies and is born again. The only escape from this dismal trap is through enlightenment. Jung says that this is no good for the Western mind, which needs to feel that it progresses towards a goal and has a purpose in its existence.

After travelling extensively in the East, Jung was eventually drawn back to study Western teachings. He realized that the study of Eastern religions had been important to him, but that it was only a part of the path that would bring him to his goal. He compared the Eastern way of thinking with that in the West and concluded that:

* Western man is mainly extraverted, finding meaning in external objects and looking for meaning in the 'real world'. Consciousness in Western man is too detached from the unconscious;

* Eastern man is mainly introverted and looks for meaning within the self. In Eastern man the tendency is for consciousness to merge completely with the unconscious.

'But,' said Jung, 'the meaning is both without and within.' He had discovered that both traditions had their own strengths and drawbacks. Neither point of view was completely right or completely wrong. This insight shows a move towards balance and maturity within Jung's own psyche – an integration of the two sides of his personality that had troubled him for so long.

CHANGES IN CHRISTIAN THINKING

Jung came to believe that Christianity was of central importance to Western man, but needed to gain new insights in order to answer the spiritual needs of modern people. 'Otherwise, it becomes out of date and date does not answer the spiritual needs of the people.' For example, he felt that there was an imbalance in the doctrine of the Trinity, which sees God as having three aspects – Father, Son and Holy Spirit. Jung felt that this idea did not acknowledge a feminine aspect to the divine. Gnostic teaching actually added a 'fourth term', as an attempt to incorporate the hidden and mysterious feminine side.

In 1950 the Catholic Church announced a new doctrine – that of the Assumption of the Virgin Mary. Jung considered this new dogma to be 'the most important religious event since the Reformation'. (*Answer to Job*) Before this, right from early times, the Church had tended to regard the feminine with deep suspicion. The problem had all begun with the doctrine of Original Sin, which says that we are all born sinful, ever since Adam and Eve ate the forbidden fruit. (Naughty wicked temptress Eve was largely responsible for this.) People began to realize that newborn babies can hardly have done anything sinful, so it must be the sexual act itself that is at the root of the problem. The Virgin Mary was exempt from this indiscretion, having produced Jesus without having to have sex. In 1950 she gained a further promotion when the doctrine of the Assumption decreed that she was taken straight up to heaven, body and spirit, when she died and didn't have to wait for the Day of Judgement like the rest of us.

Richmond Hill Public Library
Check OUT Receipt

User ID: 22971004377046

ID: 32572000108631
itle: Introducing Jung : a
graphic guide
Date due: April 3 2021 11:
59 ...

ckouts for session:

Total checkouts:13

Richmond Hill Public Library
Proudly Enriching Your
Connections, Choices and
Community.
Please return all items in
the external book drops.

Jung saw this new doctrine as being very important because he felt that it acknowledged an archetypal psychological need. Ordinary people had always shown this need in the way that they regarded the Virgin Mary as a comforting, motherly person, to whom one could pray in times of need. She had definitely been venerated all along, even though she wasn't 'officially' divine. People had visions of her too and Jung points out that she often appeared to children. 'In such cases', he said, 'the collective unconscious is always at work' (*Answer to Job*).

Jung's suggestion is that the doctrine of the Assumption is like a subconscious announcement that Mary is now being accepted as part of the Trinity, so that it becomes a 'Quaternity'. The doctrine 'expresses a renewed hope for the fulfilment of that yearning for peace which stirs deep down in the soul, and for a resolution of the threatening tension between opposites' (*Answer to Job*). Once again we have the idea of balance. Four is a more balanced number than three and Jung points out that it has often cropped up before – the four evangelists, four seasons, four elements and so on – making it a number that is archetypally satisfying. Just to be difficult, one could suggest that something is still missing from the divine group. If we have a father and a son then surely we need a daughter as well as a mother? Ought we not to have the number 5 to represent wholeness…?

Jung believed that the study of religion was very important in giving us insight into the workings of the unconscious. He stressed that when he spoke of 'God' he referred to the 'God within'. Whether or not God exists as a separate external entity was for Jung a pointless and unanswerable question. But he believed that it was essential for people to have a spiritual dimension in their lives and that numerous neuroses arose because people overlooked this aspect of their being, especially as they moved into the second half of life. People focus on the narrower aspects of life, such as work, marriage and success, but all the while they stay unhappy because they are restricting themselves spiritually. This is why Jung saw spirituality as being vitally important to the achievement of wholeness in the human psyche.

* * * *SUMMARY* * * *

• Jung saw the spiritual aspect of human experience as being of vital importance to the health of the psyche.

• He studied a wide range of different religions in order to gain insight into archetypal patterns in religious thinking.

• Jung found dogmatic fundamentalist religions unhelpful because they lead to disagreement and spiritual stagnation. He emphasized the importance of individual experience in spiritual growth.

• He believed that religions need to grow and evolve in order to answer the deep spiritual needs of ordinary people.

Conclusion

9

KEY ASPECTS OF JUNGIAN ANALYSIS

Jung emphasized that every person has a unique story to tell, some aspects of which are hidden in the unconscious. It is the unfolding of this life story that provides the pathway to individuation. Jung suggested that it is a good idea for therapists to undergo analysis themselves, to try and be aware of their own neuroses as far as possible before they begin to try and help others. It is also a good idea for therapists to have a mentor – someone more experienced than themselves, to whom they can turn for help and advice. This is because individuation is a process that we all need to go through and it is never completely finished.

The key method that Jung used during the process of analysis was always one of patiently talking with and listening to people. He discovered that this was the only way to really get to know his patients and begin to unravel their unique problems. Jung laid less emphasis on childhood experiences than other psychoanalysts had done – for him the person's life *now* was the most important aspect. He always stressed that the spiritual aspect of human psychic experience was of vital importance – he encouraged people to realize that they are not isolated beings but part of a great mysterious whole.

The system of psychology that Jung developed over the years provided him with a useful map of the psyche and gave structure to his therapy sessions. He used various different approaches to finding his way into a person's inner world.

Symbols

Jung encouraged his patients to talk about their dreams and fantasies and to explore their symbolic content. These symbolic messages provided clues as to what was going on in the person's unconscious. By discussing symbols and a person's emotional reactions towards them, Jung found that he could often bring unconscious material into conscious awareness and so begin to reach what was really bothering a person.

Archetypal messages

Many symbolic messages that emerge from the unconscious turn out to be archetypal in nature. Jung often worked with these symbols in a constructive way, using a process of **amplification**. This meant that he would discuss possible connections with symbolism in myth, folklore and religion, in order to arrive at clarification and enhanced meaning. He was exploring the collective content of dreams and fantasies, rather than just interpreting them from an individual viewpoint.

KEYWORDS

Amplification: exploring symbolic meanings by comparisons with myth, folklore and religion.

Transcendent function: a new, more healthy attitude that emerges in the psyche when two opposite functions become integrated.

Association

Given an original image or idea, Jung would encourage the patient to follow a train of spontaneous connected thoughts. He believed that these were always meaningful in one way or another, and might uncover unconscious complexes.

Active imagination

Jung encouraged people to explore symbolism emerging from the unconscious in creative ways such as drawing, painting, drama or writing. This active imagination process is like play and brings the person back to a child-like state that allows the unconscious to express itself more freely.

Balancing of opposites

Jung frequently emphasized the process of the balancing of opposites, which is necessary to achieve a healthy integrated psyche. Once two conflicting opposite trends are brought into consciousness the tension between them can be resolved. A third state, representing a new, more healthy attitude can now emerge. Jung called this third state the **transcendent function**.

JUNG'S VISION

For Jung, life was a sacred journey with meaning and purpose. His interests were very wide-ranging and he wrote extensively upon many different subjects. Above all, he was a psychologist and analyst, and it is this aspect of his work that most people come to first. His analytical method gradually strips away built-up defensive layers of the personality until we are able to see our true selves. The goal is to achieve a wider, fuller consciousness, less dependent upon ego. This new consciousness is no longer totally egocentric, obsessed with its own petty needs and endlessly using unconscious ploys to cover up its inadequacies.

Like all great thinkers, Jung has had plenty of critics. Some of them have accused him of being domineering and egotistical, determined to collect devoted admirers in the academic world. Some have pointed out his selfish side – saying that he lived off his wife's fortune and was a frightful womanizer. Still others have accused him of anti-Semitism and debate still rages about the nature of his involvement with the Nazis. Certainly he was not a perfect being, but really this only serves to make him more human – like all of us he had his shadow side. But whatever he was like as a person, it is certainly true that his influence has extended far beyond his work as a psychologist, making him one of the greatest thinkers of the twentieth century.

* His ideas about the collective unconscious and archetypes have given us new insights into the history of the human psyche.

* His life-long interest in dreams has expanded our understanding of the mysterious world of the unconscious.

* Many of his ideas about personality, such as introversion and extra-version, have become part of everyday language and understanding.

* His fascination with mythology, religion and the paranormal has encouraged people to open up new thinking about spiritual psychology.

* Jungian analysts are now trained all over the world and there are many institutions devoted to expanding his ideas.

Jung's psychology has been attacked for encouraging people to concentrate mostly upon the self – critics say that he does not give enough attention to relationships with others. Jung argues that we cannot hope to relate well to others until we can see ourselves clearly. He says that it is not in fact possible to separate the relationship with the self from the relationship with others. It is impossible to relate properly to other people until we can relate to ourselves.

Jung's charismatic personality has inspired many people and taught us to look deeply within ourselves and begin to accept ourselves for who we truly are. Ultimately this is a spiritual journey – one that Jung himself saw as being essential if mankind were to have a future. It is this conscious awareness and fulfilment of one's own unique being – the individuation process – that is the pathway and the goal of Jungian analysis.

GLOSSARY

Alchemy An esoteric practice combining aspects of mysticism, magic, science and religion.

Amplification Exploring symbolic meanings by comparisons with myth, folklore and religion.

Analytical Studying things by breaking them down into their separate elements.

Anima The unconscious feminine side of a man's personality.

Animus The unconscious masculine side of a woman's personality.

Archetype A recurring image or pattern of thinking which represents a typical human experience.

Astrology Study of the ways in which celestial bodies affect human affairs.

Causality The idea that related events are connected by cause and effect.

Collective unconscious The deepest layer of the unconscious, which extends beyond the individual psyche.

Complex A related group of emotionally charged unconscious ideas.

Divination Insight into the future or the unknown, gained by paranormal methods.

Dogma Principle beliefs laid down by religious authorities.

Ego The centre of consciousness and the sense of identity.

Eight psychological types Combination of the four personality types and the two attitudes (introversion and extraversion).

Equinoxes Days (two a year) on which day and night are of equal length.

Esoteric Secret or mystical knowledge, revealed only to those 'in the know'.

Extraversion Direction of interest outwards towards external objects and relationships. Also extroversion.

Four functions Four basic personality types.

Fundamentalist Strict adherence to ancient doctrines and texts of a religion.

Gnostic Relating to knowledge, especially occult mystical knowledge.

I Ching Ancient Chinese method of divination.

Individuation Conscious realization and fulfilment of the self.

Introversion Direction of interest inwards towards the inner world of thoughts and feelings.

Intuitive Knowing things without having to reason them out.

Libido Motivating psychic energy.

Mandala A symbolic circular figure that represents the universe or the wholeness of the self.

Mechanistic View that sees a person as a machine whose behaviour is determined by physical or chemical causes.

Mythopoeic To do with the making of myths.

Myths Traditional stories that try to explain natural, social or religious ideas.

Natal chart Chart showing the position of the celestial bodies at the time of someone's birth.

Neurosis Minor nervous or mental disorder.

Numinous Awe-inspiring; indicating the presence of the divine.

Objective To do with, or coming from, the external world.

Occult Secret knowledge, concerning the mysterious, paranormal or magical.

Paranormal Things that cannot be explained by normal, objective methods.

Parapsychology The study of paranormal mental phenomena.

Persona The public face that a person assumes when relating to others.

Philosophy A system of learning that investigates the underlying nature and truth of knowledge and existence.

Positivism A way of thinking that limits knowledge to that which is directly observable.

Precognition Knowing something in advance, often by paranormal means.

Primeval Ancient or primitive.

Projection Process whereby an unconscious characteristic, a fault, or even a talent of one's own is seen as belonging to another person or object.

Psyche The mind, soul or spirit.

Psychiatrist Someone who studies and treats mental and nervous disorders.

Psychoanalysis A system of psychology and method of treating mental disorders, originally developed by Freud.

Psychogenic Disorders that originate with mental conditions – physical symptoms may follow on.

Psychokinesis Moving things by mental effort, without using any known natural force.

Psychologist Scientist who studies the mind and behaviour.

Psychotic Suffering from severe mental disorder.

Repressed Experiences that have been actively pushed out of the conscious mind into the unconscious.

Self The archetype of wholeness of the psyche which transcends the ego.

Shadow The unconscious part of the personality that contains characteristics which one cannot recognize as one's own.

Shamanic Relating to ancient, tribal, spiritual practices.

Subjective To do with, or coming from, the self.

Synchronicity The simultaneous occurrence of two meaningful but not causally connected events.

Transcendent function A new, more healthy attitude that emerges in the psyche when two opposite functions become integrated.

Transference Emotional involvement between patient and therapist.

Unconscious Parts of the mind and personality of which a person is unaware.

Word association Process where a patient is given a word and then tells the analysts all the ideas that spontaneously come to mind.

Yin and Yang The two balances and opposite principles that operate in the universe according to Chinese philosophy.

Yoga Hindu system of philosophy involving meditation, physical exercises and other spiritual practices.

Zeitgeist The spirit of the age.

FURTHER READING

There are huge numbers of books available both by and about Jung
The following brief list offers a few suggestions about where to begin
further reading.

Books written by Jung:

* *Memories, Dreams, Reflections*, Fontana, 1967.
  This is Jung's autobiography, recorded and edited by his secretary
  Aniela Jaffe. It is one of the best introductions to Jung.

* *Modern Man in Search of a Soul*, Routledge, 1933

* *Man and His Symbols*, Picador, 1978

Books about Jung:

* *Carl Gustav Jung*, Frank McLynn, Bantam Press, 1996

* *An Introduction to Jung's Psychology*, Frieda Fordham, Penguin
  1991

* *On Jung*, Anthony Stevens, Penguin, 1991

A useful guide around Jung's extensive works is:

* *A Guided Tour of the Collected Works of C G Jung*, Robert H
  Hopcke, Shambala, 1989

Website

Another invaluable resource is the following web page:

* **http://www.cgjung.com**

FREUD –
A BEGINNER'S GUIDE

Ruth Berry

Freud – A Beginner's Guide introduces you to the 'father of psychoanalysis' and his work. No need to wrestle with difficult concepts as key ideas are presented in a clear and jargon-free way.

Ruth Berry's informative text explores:

- Freud's background and the times he lived in
- the development of psychoanalysis
- the ideas surrounding Freud's work on the unconscious.

The facts … the concepts … the ideas …

EINSTEIN –
A BEGINNER'S GUIDE

Jim Breithaupt

Einstein – A Beginner's Guide introduces you to the great scientist and his work. No need to wrestle with difficult concepts as key ideas are presented in a clear and jargon-free way.

Jim Breithaupt's lively text:

- presents Einstein's work in historical context
- sets out the experimental evidence in support of Einstein's theories
- takes you through the theory of relativity, in simple terms
- describes the predictions from Einstein's theories on the future of the universe.

The facts ... the concepts ... the ideas ...